LIFE IN

THE

PAST

LANE

BY

LARRY
VANDEVENTER

ISBN: 1-4033-5926-1 (e-book)
ISBN: 1-4033-5927-X (Paperback)

This book is printed on acid free paper.

1stBooks - rev. 01/24/03

To

Regina

Dedication and Acknowledgements

This book is dedicated to Audrey Grace Carter our first grandchild and the firstborn of our daughter TM and son-in-law Todd. Audrey developed her own timeline and arrived two and one-half months early but she was still strong enough to wrap herself around several fingers and get her way. At this writing she is one year old and she is a healthy, happy typical girl.

I also wish to acknowledge Anna Rochelle, Editor of the Worthington Times and Chris Pruett, Editor of the Linton Daily Citizen who have given me an outlet for my writing.

I also wish to acknowledge the many people who have written, called, sent email messages and who have spoken to me about how much they enjoy reading the column. Their encouragement has been very important to me as well as an incentive to continue writing. Thank you.

Best Wishes

Larry Vandeventer

Also author of
Bumps In The Road [Things I Have Run Across]

TABLE OF CONTENTS

Introduction

Of the writing of books there is no end. Thousands of books are published every year. Why should you read this book? It will remind you that life can be good. Life is meant to be lived in joy. There are millions of good people in the world who are the adhesive that holds life together. Sometimes we forget about that and allow ourselves to be swallowed by the negative aspects of life.

Be assured that I am no Pollyanna. There are bad people in the world and bad things do happen to good people. I choose not to dwell on the negative and I choose to accentuate the positive.

This book is comprised of stories that are filled with wisdom, wit and wistfulness. They will remind you of the goodness of life. I was born and grew up on a farm near Ghost Hollow, Indiana, and have pursued several career options as a minister, public educator and university professor. In my life of service and learning I have observed many things to share with you.

I firmly believe you will enjoy reading this book. It will make your day a bit brighter, lighten your step and cause you to review your daily attitudes and outlook. I guarantee it.

By the way, you will need to know that BW is my wife, TW and TM are my daughters. You will be left to determine what they letters mean. I will never reveal the meanings unless you offer me a substantial sum of money. I value my life too much.

What Others Say About the Book

"Definitely comic, assuredly a heart string tugger, reading Larry Vandeventer's, *Life in the Past Lane*, will stick in your store of special memories because you've either been there or you are on your way. Among Indiana Authors he stands tall and out." [Larry Incollingo, Author and columnist for the Bloomington Herald-Times.]

"Readers look forward to his column. Vandeventer's writing is very Middle America. He is able to put into words the way small town people feel the Bumps in the Road." [Anna Rochelle, Editor, Worthington Times.]

"Larry Vandeventer introduces us to a cast of delightful bucolic characters — "Geezers," he calls them — who make us forget the perils of the moment. Relax in an old rocking chair and return to a time when life was less complex, friendship more genuine and humor was tasteful, not trenchant." [Wendell Trogdon, Author, Retired Managing Editor and Columnist for the Indianapolis News.]

"Larry Vandeventer has a way of taking the reader back into his childhood days in the Calvertville and Worthington areas. From start to finish he does a good job of capturing his thoughts and passing them on to the reader with a mix of comedy and seriousness. His columns have become a popular addition to our publication." [Chris Pruett, Editor/General Manager, Linton Daily Citizen.]

There Is Never Enough Batter Left In The Bowl

Ever since I can remember I have liked to eat cake batter and cookie dough. My all time favorite is white cake. From the days of my youth when my mother baked cakes to the present day I have never had enough batter. There is never enough batter left in the bowl.

When my children, TW and TM, were at home, I had to compete with them which left me with very meager portions. When I complained to management, BW, I got the stock answer that the cake would not rise properly if more batter were left out. I never accepted that answer but you can't fight city hall. The meager amount that I received reminded me of the paltry amount of swill the kids got in Oliver Twist.

One day I decided that I had suffered enough. I determined that my deprivation must end and that my need for a sufficient quantity of cake batter must be fulfilled. My body cried out for more. My mind could not be content unless drastic actions were taken. My inner need for that delicacy longed for satiation. My tongue craved batter and more batter. The meager quantity that is traditionally left in the customary bowl no longer slaked my appetite for that smooth viscous ambrosia that twirled musically on my tongue, then slid effortlessly down my esophagus to my tummy where it segued into my bloodstream and sent a message to my brain that shouted, "this is good stuff."

Taking matters into my own hands, throwing caution to the wind, propelling myself with reckless abandon I purchased a cake mix and began my pilgrimage to paradise. I rummaged around in the cabinet and found a suitable glass-mixing bowl into which I poured the contents of the white cake mix. Then I added the requisite egg, water and a bit of oil as required in the directions. Next, I found the mixer and commenced to mix. After just a few minutes of whirring and whipping, the batter was ready. As I gazed at it, I began to salivate. My lips could barely hold back the floodtide as my anticipation grew to Matterhorn dimensions. Only a Herculean swallowing effort prevented a salivary "boo-boo" on the counter.

My prize was ready. The bowl was nearly full. I removed the beaters and flippantly discarded them in the sink. Normally I lick them to get every tiny morsel of batter. Today they were insignificant compared to the bounty of batter in the bowl. Usually BW brings the bowl with its pitiful remnant of batter clinging desperately to the sides and the lip, the beaters and a spatula as my eating tool. None of that today. I ceremoniously took the bowl and its heavenly contents and a tablespoon and went out on the patio where I could consume my ambrosia while communing with nature.

I took a seat in the swing that is nestled in the shade of a huge Tulip tree beside the patio, and contemplated briefly on the delicious prize before me. Then I plunged that tablespoon deeply into the magic elixir filling it to where it could hold no more and then placed it into my mouth where my tongue was making moves that Ricky Martin can only dream about. My taste buds were having a block party with a live band and dancing. I savored the flavor. I was making noises like the wine steward in a swanky restaurant or the judge at the annual wine festival in Napa Valley. I was addicted and unafraid.

As if it had a mind of its own, the spoon found its way back to the bowl and then into my mouth many times. My head was swooning with each spoonfull that entered my mouth. My body cried out for more. My mind was not content and demanded more. My inner need for that delicacy still longed for satiation. My tongue craved batter and more batter. Finally, I was getting all of the batter that I craved. Now I understood more fully how the drug pusher hooks his victims and then becomes the supplier.

As I sat there in the shade, slurping and smacking, and listening to the chirping birds and enjoying the lovely flowers, I slowly became aware of a change. Slowly but surely another reality began to creep into my awareness. The craving for batter was quickly becoming satisfied. The transition time for the spoon, that batter conveyer belt, was noticeably much slower. My tongue was no longer dancing with joy. My brain was sending the subtle message that just maybe I had had enough batter. Heresy! I have never had enough batter. "Press onward," cried my batter induced taste buds, however weakly.

The batter that once tasted of ambrosia now had a slick taste to it. The consistency was the same but it seemed thicker in my mouth and my salivary glands were now working overtime just to provide enough moisture to prevent the batter from congealing in my mouth.

I thought that I could eat the batter of at least three cake mixes but now the reality of it was that after about ten or fewer large spoons of the delicacy I realized that maybe my craving had been satisfied. Humbled by that reality, I checked the bowl contents. It contained more than 97% of the original content. Even though it seemed that I had eaten gallons of the batter, the contents of the bowl seemed as full as when I began. How could that be? What was wrong with the picture? Were my senses deluded? Were my eyes larger than my stomach as my mother used to say?

The remainder of the batter was baked into a delicious cake. I concluded that there is nothing better than batter but too much batter can get the better of you. I wonder how brownie batter would taste?

The Empty Mail Box

Today is one of those winter days in Indiana that tend to cause Hoosiers to have bouts of depression. A huge gray canvas has been drawn over the sky covering the landscape and hiding the sun. The overcast is as impenetrable as kryptonite. Superman could not penetrate it. The landscape is in the annual dormant stage of winter. The trees and vegetation are all taking a break. What isn't brown is black or dirty brown. The grass is brown. Weeds and underbrush have given up and in a brown state of mind await the coming of spring that is at least three months away. The only color is the evergreen trees that dot the landscape. The trees dropped their leaves long ago and they stand naked and mute against the leaden, brooding sky. They look embarrassed as I gaze upon their bare limbs. They sigh deeply as the cold, blustery, winter wind rips through their branches.

I was driving on such a day on Indiana 67 and my thoughts were enveloped in a melancholy gloom. The persistent rainfall from the sinister clouds intensified my melancholy. Those clouds seem to be just about three feet higher than the tallest trees. I had the feeling that I was driving through a gloomy, ominous tunnel with no light at the end. The constant beating of the windshield wipers keep time with the gloominess playing on the tape deck in my mind.

The temperature was not horribly cold but the combination of wind and rain made me shiver even though I was warm and secure inside my car. The rain pounded on the roof and windows of the car in a vain attempt to get inside. The wind huffed and puffed and tried to blow the car off the road. Passing cars and trucks splashed water and dirt from the road on the windshield momentarily obscuring my vision until the wipers could clean it off.

I was reflecting on the reality that nearly all of the old homesteads of my youth are gone. More modern houses have replaced a few of the houses. But most of the old houses have either burned, been torn down or they sit in various stages of decay. They have disappeared like smoke in the winds of time. The old barns and out buildings have moldered into the ground and disappeared. The old familiar landmarks have evanesced - vanished like steam - into antiquity. The people who now live in the neighbor-hood are strangers to me.

The heavy rain pounded on the car roof and windows, the tattoo harsh and unrelenting. The staccato beat maintained the steady rhythm as I continued on my way. For some unknown reason my gaze was diverted to my left. My attention came to rest on a small knoll and through the lonely rain I could see an old, long abandoned farmstead. It was in a sad state of disrepair. I speculated that the house and barn were built in the early part of the 20th century or the latter part of the 19th century. It looked as if the farmstead has been vacant for many years.

I stopped beside the road to spend some time in contemplation. The house was a lifeless, listless relic of years gone by. It stared forlornly down at me through lifeless eyes of broken glass. The driving rain made the house look even more sad and alone. In one window the tattered remnant of a curtain flapped in the wind waving desperately to gain my attention. The windows reminded me of the lifeless eyes of a deer that had lost a battle with an eighteen-wheeler. There was no activity, no sign of life. As the wind and rain bullied their way through the house and barn, they cried and mourned for the long ago when a man farmed the land, a woman kept the house and their joyful children played around in the yard.

There was an old barn with a small silo standing guard at its side. The barn doors drooped and sagged hanging desperately by one hinge. The metal roof flopped and

5

rattled in the wind, clinging desperately to the rafters hoping against hope that someone would come to repair it so it could regain its rightful place as the guardian against intruding rain and snow. The garden spot was overgrown with weeds and brush. The yard is now home to groundhogs, rabbits and birds. It will never again be a neatly trimmed playground for laughing children and a place where adults would visit. The farmstead that once was a vibrant place filled with life, now slumped listlessly in the driving rain. Abandoned and alone.

In my reverie I wondered where the people are who last lived there. The parents have probably joined their ancestors in the city of the dead. The children have likely scattered like confetti before the wind to the four corners of the state and nation. The grandchildren and great grandchildren will never come to that place. It stood there in agonizing silence hoping, longing that someone would visit once again.

In my mind's eye the last days of habitation in the old farmstead played out like a television program. I saw an old woman, with the years pressing down on her frail body, saying a tearful goodbye to the place where she had lived for so many years. Her face was crinkled like a crumpled piece of paper. As the children waited impatiently for her, she took one more walk through the house of memories.

As she stopped in the kitchen she sees her family gathered to eat and to share the events of the day. She sees her small children waking up in their upstairs bedrooms and she hears them come tumbling down the narrow stairs, bursting into the warmth of the kitchen. They would gather around the table like birds in the nest waiting for their mother to feed them. She remembered the wood burning stove, later replaced by an electric stove, where she prepared hundreds of meals. The aroma of baking ham and biscuits prodded her memory and brought a faint smile.

The crows' feet beside her eyes deepened as she contemplated those days.

She saw her beloved Frank coming in from the barn with fresh milk and eggs. A vision of family and friends who tended to gather in the kitchen floated through the mists of her memory. The aroma of baking turkey, yeast bread fresh out of the oven, perking coffee, boiling vegetables and fresh pies cooling in the pie safe wafted through the quiet room. She recalled the many joyous times when people talked and laughed around the kitchen table. She also remembered how she and Frank and the children sat around that same table and ironed out the wrinkles of conflict and trouble that often creased the fabric of their lives.

Then she stopped for a few minutes in the bedroom where she and her love had snuggled together for warmth during that first November night that they spent in the house. The baby crib was placed in that room next to their bed and the babies slept peacefully by their side. It was also a nursery where they came when they didn't feel well. She could not keep from smiling as she remembered the pitter-patter of little feet as four frightened kids raced to get in bed with them to wait out the summer storms. That bed was a place of refuge when the summer electrical storms thundered and crashed through the countryside. How safe and snug they all felt together while the storm tried to scare them.

The next stop was the living room where the family and friends gathered to visit and to play games such as dominos, checkers, marbles and Piggly Wiggly. They read the stories of the Bible, Mother Goose Nursery Rhymes and Old Fashioned Fairy Tales. They gathered around the old pump organ and sang songs while the kerosene lamps gave the room a yellowish glow. She saw the tranquil nights when she and her Frank quietly talked or read the newspaper.

Glancing out of the window she saw the garden where the family worked to grow the vegetables that they ate fresh during the summer and later canned to eat through the long winter until the garden produced again the next year. She smelled the fresh earth as Frank plowed the ground for the spring planting. She remembered how the fresh earth felt as she walked barefoot through it. She could hear the children grumbling about having to help plant and hoe the garden but she also remembered how they loved to eat the produce from the garden in the depths of winter. How wonderful it would be, she thought, to sit down once again at the table laden with homegrown corn, beans, potatoes and tomatoes. She longed to hear little Bobby say once again, "I'm so full that I think I am going to bust!" Little Bobby now has children in high school and lives two states away.

To the right of the garden spot is the barn where Frank and the boys stored the hay to feed the animals. They milked the cows twice a day every day to slake the milk thirst of six people the year around. She remembered that each year they would confine a beef cow in that barn and feed it until it reached the right size to butcher. Then on a clear cold December day they butchered the animal for their meat supply. They also butchered a hog each year. She smelled the fire under the huge black kettle as the lard is cooked out of the cracklins. Family and neighbors would work together to prepare the meat for eating. She heard Frank calling the cows to come home in the gathering dusk of a summer evening. She heard the clucking chickens and grunting pigs that were also a part of farming.

The last stop was the front porch. She sensed that her daughter and son-in-law were growing restless as they waited for her, however, she had to linger a little longer. The porch is where people congregated in the summer to escape the heat of the day. There was a swing where she and Frank liked to rest after the day's toil. Even now she felt the warm gentle breeze in her hair as they sat together.

8

Wooden rocking chairs also provided a place to sit. The children spent many hours in the swing often hitting the house in their rambunctious efforts to entertain themselves. When the girls courted they sat there with their dates to talk and dream of the future. It was the same swing where grandpa and grandma sat and reminisced about the good old days. The porch was a classroom where the kids learned from their elders about life and what it meant to be a mother, father, male, female, and member of the community. In that same swing she had to come to grips with living alone again.

Today, however, is the last day that she would live in the house that had been her home for over fifty years. A void came to dwell in her heart that could never be filled. On the loneliest day of her life, her beloved Frank had passed away a few years ago. She had watched her grandparents pass from this life. Then she had watched her parents, uncles and aunts and other family members leave this life of toil and pain. Then her beloved Frank was gone. She just could not imagine life without him.

She continued to live on the farm but now she just couldn't keep the place up anymore and take care of her personal needs. Her daughter and husband waited to take her to live with them in another state. The other children had already helped in the auction sale that disposed of the last of the farm equipment and the unneeded household items. As the children waited somewhat impatiently, she was lost in reverie. The vermillion-colored sun was going down behind the trees. Gusts of wind blew around the house and through the yard; leaves swirled around her feet. A rabbit scampered through the yard and into the garden. Geese honked forlornly as they winged their way South. A hoot owl hooted plaintively from the edge of the woods. The first grip of cool night air nipped at her ears and nose. She shivered and pulled her coat tighter around her shoulders.

"Are you ready, mom?" her daughter asked quietly. "Yes", she heard herself reply in a quiet mournful voice, the word fought the wind struggling to reach their ears. She got into the car as tears of sadness quietly coursed down her weathered face. As the car reached the end of the lane she quietly said, "Please, stop a moment." She got out of the car to take one last long look at the old place. After a lingering, pensive look, through tear filled eyes that strained to remember everything they saw, her mind buried deeply in reverie, she crossed the road to check the mailbox. She pulled the door open and it was empty, as empty as the old house and the huge hole in her heart. She got back into the car and they left the old place never to return.

Big Ben Isn't So Big Now

Recently I was rummaging around through some stuff in the bottom of my closet and found a small alarm clock with the brand name of Big Ben. The back was black, the face was white and the rim and stand were chrome. Several buttons and keys protruded from the back. There was one to wind it, one to set the time, one to set the alarm hand to one to pull out so the alarm bell would ring at the appointed time. Immediately I recognized it as the clock that my dad faithfully wound and set on the shelf in the kitchen every evening before he went to bed. He had given it to me many years ago and I had forgotten that I had it.

Instantaneously I was swept away on the winds of nostalgia to a country kitchen with a wood burning cook stove and a pitcher pump in the sink. An ice box sat in the corner and a table and chairs sat at the south end. My mom prepared hundreds of wonderful meals in that room. This was a place where my parents and we three kids sat down together and ate three meals every day of our lives. You get to know people rather well when you do that. Would that the five us could sit around the table again as we did so long ago.

Every evening before he went to bed, dad would take Big Ben down from a shelf, wind him and the alarm, pull the alarm button out and replace it on the shelf. Big Ben would tick tock all night in the dark and faithfully jingle and jangle the next morning at 5:00 a.m. Dad would roll out of bed, do his chores, eat breakfast and then drive to Bloomington or Crane and work as a carpenter.

I remember the clock as being quite large. Today it is quite small and fits easily in my hand. What changed. I wound him up and sat and listened to Ben tick for awhile. Once again I was a little kid in the kitchen watching my dad wind Big Ben. Ben doesn't seem as big now.

11

As a kid growing up on a farm in Southern Indiana, I heard my parents and others talk about places in far off lands around the world. They talked about places "Across the water" or "Across the Big Pond" usually meaning the Atlantic Ocean. Since most Americans were Eurocentric they rarely spoke of the Pacific Ocean and the Pacific Rim. They talked about London, England, Paris, Moscow and China. I remember listening and wondering where those places were. As I grew and learned more about such places, I dreamed of going there. I wanted to see how the people looked and how they lived. I wondered if they lived a better life that we did.

Many years have passed since that overall-clad rag-a-muffin kid dreamed of seeing places around the world. The U.S. Navy took me to some of those places, i.e., Florida, New York, Boston, Norfolk and Newfoundland but not those more exotic places. Finally, BW and I saved our lunch and egg money, took the plunge and went on a European tour. One of the places we stopped was London, England. We went on several tours and saw many places that I have always heard about and dreamed of seeing.

One site we passed and where we took several pictures was the Big Ben Clock Tower at the house of parliament. The tour guide said the place was not named for the clock but the Tower itself. Or was it the other way around.

As we stood there looking at Big Ben, I was thinking about the clock that dad wound each night and wishing that I were back in the warm kitchen so I could talk to him again.

The Magic of the Marathon

When you live in the country, a town is a special place. I grew up on the farm back in the 1940's and 50's in Southern Indiana. We were isolated from the mainstream of life, but it was an idyllic life and I loved it. However, on the farm you spend much of your time with the same people day after day. General farming, as we lived, is a consuming enterprise. Back then country people had limited opportunities to visit and socialize. We raised chickens, pigs, beef cattle and dairy cattle that required milking twice a day every day. We also grew corn, beans and hay that required tending and a huge garden.

There were always weeds to cut, fences to build and mend, gates to repair, buildings to maintain, equipment to keep in good condition, household work, cooking, crops to tend and harvest and the list goes on and on. All of that enterprise consumed our lives and didn't leave much time to go to town or to just hang out. Our family seldom left the county and never went on a vacation. I never missed it because I had never been on a vacation anyway.

Towns held a special interest to country folks back then and to a lesser degree today. It is true that many feel that town is a good place to visit but not necessarily a good place to live. There are various kinds of activity in towns. A town means action. A town means people. A town means business activity. A town means opportunity to see and be seen. People are engaged in many enterprises. It all seems more exciting and interesting than living in the country. I felt that way too.

In my hometown of Worthington, Indiana, the Marathon Inn was a magical place. This was long before the Interstate System was in place. As I remember the Terrells owned and operated the business that was a combination filling station and restaurant. During the day that building was a bustling oasis where people stopped to refuel their cars and themselves. It seemed to me that most of the natives ate at the Busy Bee Restaurant or the Triangle Restaurant. Customers at the Marathon were out-of-towners.

It seems so surreal now but when I was growing up, we never ate in a restaurant. Restaurants were like nirvana to me. It wasn't until I was in junior high or high school that I would buy burgers and fries and milk shakes in restaurants. I don't remember our family ever going to a restaurant for a meal while I was living at home. The first time I saw my dad eating french fries and a burger at Rawley's Sandwich Shop, it seemed very strange indeed to me.

Most of the clientele at the Marathon were from out of town. In the summer it was a place of respite from the heat of traveling in the car or truck with no air conditioning. It was a place to get a cool drink and stretch your legs. In the winter it was a warm place to escape the icy breath of Old Man Winter. During the night, it was a haven of light that all of the darkness in the world could not snuff out.

The Marathon, as we called it, was located on the north side of town where highway 67 curved northward toward Freedom, Spencer and Indianapolis. Cars from Michigan, Kentucky, Tennessee, Ohio, Illinois and other states could be seen parked around the station. The gas pumps were situated on an angle just off the highway somewhat like pit road at the Indy 500. Cars would turn in off the highway, refuel at the pumps and then move off into traffic. Huge trucks slid into the station like mammoth black whales and snuggled up to a diesel pumping umbilical cord for sustenance. There was a grease rack or lift outside the building where cars were serviced. It doesn't seem that it was used much and I speculate that the owners made most of their money on the sale of gasoline, diesel fuel and oil. It appeared to be an exciting place to work.

Men from the community and some of the older teenagers worked there. That looked like a great job. They would hustle out of the station with a smile and a spiffy shirt with their name on it. They would always greet you and say, "fill'er up?" If you said yes or no just two dollars worth, they would ask, "Ethyl or Regular?" The attendant would then turn a crank on the side of the pump to reset it and then flip up the lever where the nozzle was housed. Those old pumps had nozzles with a lever that had to be held down in a gripping motion to release the gas. There was no special attachment or device to hold it "on." Just as today, the gas would stop flowing unless that lever was held down. There were tricks to the trade though.

The enterprising workers removed the gas cap from the car and use it as a chock to hold the handle while they tended the car. While the fuel was being pumped, they would always check the oil, check the air pressure in your tires, wash the windshield, check the water level in the radiator and battery and inspect the belts and hoses under the hood. Then they would take the money and send you on the way with a thank you, a smile and a pleasant "come back." That is why it was called a service station. The traveler would truly receive service.

Summer nights around the station held a certain loneliness that gave rise to strange imaginings. I would imagine where the people were going. My mind would envision that they were going to exotic places that I had never seen or even heard of. I would imagine what they did for a living which undoubtedly was more interesting and exciting than farming. I would imagine that they were traveling to engage in dynamic activities or enterprise that did not exist in Calvertville. I could visualize the places where they lived and in the pages of my mind those places were much more exotic, lively and fascinating than Calvertville or Worthington. Their lives seemed to be so much more interesting than mine.

Cars and trucks would come in out of the darkness like a dog looking for a hot meal. They would fill up at the pumps and be on their way. They would leave town traveling North over the iron bridge that spanned Eel River, through the hills toward Indianapolis. Or they would travel South through the prairie land toward Vincennes and Evansville. The darkness would swallow them and they would never be seen again. How I wished to go with them and travel to different places, to see more of the world than Greene County, Indiana.

I remember that the Marathon was also the bus stop for the Indianapolis to Vincennes (IV) line. I thought driving a bus must be a really neat job also. He got to wear a spiffy uniform with shiny shoes and a tie and a military looking hat. The driver would meet and see many different people every day. More than that he got to see the country, at least more of the country than Highland Township, Greene County.

When BW and I were in our first year of marriage we lived in Indianapolis. One time we were returning to Indy on a Sunday evening and out of necessity stopped at the Marathon for gas. A lady was there who needed a ride. She was selling velvet pictures long before there was a velvet Elvis. We took her all the way to the city for which she thanked us profusely. I'm not sure that I would do that today.

When BW was going to college in Indy, sometimes on Sunday evenings I would take her to the Marathon where she caught a ride with other college students who were attending Butler University.

Working at the Marathon did look very exciting to a teenage kid. The truth is that. later on I worked in a couple of gas stations and it was interesting, noble and honorable, but far from exciting. I also learned that those people passing through were mostly people just like everyone else. Their lives and work were hardly more exciting or interesting than mine. It just looked like it to a pilgrim who was tied to a certain place. But I received an education while I worked there.

I learned five things while working in a service station. First, it is hard work and you get tired. Second, you get your hands greasy and your clothes dirty. Third, people always need gas when it is raining really hard. Fourth, you freeze your biscuit off in the winter and sweat it off in the summer. And, fifth, I learned that there was only one thing I wanted to get out of working in a service station — me.

Amy Danced with Old Man Blizzard

Amy was a traveling sales representative who worked for a company in Terre Haute, Indiana. Her territory required her to travel by herself throughout Western Indiana and Eastern Illinois. She sold audiovisual equipment and supplies and called on school districts.

Amy was a drop dead gorgeous girl of 24 and a graduate of Indiana State University. Besides being very attractive, she was gregarious, funny and an effective sales representative. As we talked I remarked that she was the same age as my oldest daughter and I would be very worried and concerned about her safety knowing that she traveled alone, ate alone and stayed in motels alone several nights each week. She said that she had a routine and stayed in the same places all the time and felt quite safe.

I asked her if she ever had any times when she felt threatened. She told me about one time in the depths of winter she was on the far western sector of her territory in Effingham, Illinois. A snowstorm was predicted to begin later in the day or early evening. Then the predictions changed to winter storm watch and then winter storm warning. By mid-afternoon blizzard warnings were broadcast. She decided to go home to Terre Haute feeling confident she would reach home before the blizzard hit.

So at 4:00 she took the on ramp for I-70 and started East. The sky was deeply overcast and ominous looking and the wind was already blowing very hard. Snowflakes began to swirl around the car after a few minutes of travel and she noticed very little traffic. The farther she went, the fewer vehicles she saw.

After about 30 minutes, the sky was so leaden and low that visibility was extremely limited. The snow now was very heavy and the wind was blowing at near gale levels. Radio stations were advising people not to travel and to find a place of shelter. The flakes were huge and very wet.

Amy pressed on; her lights fought a losing battle with the snow and darkness. The wind was so heavy and so fierce that whiteouts made visibility impossible at times. The wiper blades were struggling to keep the heavy snow off the windshield. The sky now looked like a blanket had been pulled over the horizon. Traction was difficult.

The car was slipping and sliding along the road surface, the tires bit into the snow trying to maintain a grip on the road. In the prairie land of Illinois, there is nothing to break the full force of the wind.

The snow then came so heavily that the windshield wipers could not keep it off. Amy's mouth was dry, her neck was tense. Her stomach was turning cartwheels that an Olympic gymnast would envy. She could taste the fear welling up within her. The ice and snow accumulated on the windshield making it all but impossible to see. She had to stop and clean it off.

She stopped under an overpass to provide a bit of protection. The blinding snowstorm made it very difficult to see road signs or other landmarks. Panic came in and sat down beside her. She left the engine running and got out to clean the windshield and headlights. As she turned to get back into the car the wind ripped at her coat. She had left the door ajar to be sure it did not freeze shut and so that she could get in quickly. She reached for the door, her feet slipped and she fell against the door. It slammed shut.

She yanked on the handle and in that heartbreaking moment she realized that she was locked out. Hoping against hope, she yanked again. It was locked. She struggled through the deep drifting snow and the howling wind to the other side and tried that door. It was locked also. Despair and fear walked up and looked her straight in the eyes. The car mocked her as it sat there with the engine running, the lights on and the heater keeping the inside very snug and warm. The car was locked tighter than Scrooge's wallet. Panic struck her heart. Desperately she felt in her pockets for a key. She vainly tried to open the hood and the trunk.

The snow was intensifying and in the howling wind, it was blowing sideways. Now it was quite dark and the temperature was dropping quickly. There was no traffic. The wind moaned and groaned around the car and underpass. Desperation crept into the pages of her mind. She desperately looked for a nearby house. There was nothing.

Several minutes passed and she became colder and more desperate. Her coat and hair were covered in snow. Despondently she tried to keep moving, stamping her feet and flexing her arms in a vain attempt to keep warm. The irony was that she was standing beside a car that was running with the heater operating at maximum and she could not get inside. She was about to give up when suddenly out of the maelstrom of snow and ice a ghostly apparition plowed through the blizzard. She was afraid to look, because at first she thought that it was an optical illusion. But the illusion materialized into a four by four pickup truck with huge tires.

The truck stopped. The driver, a young man about 20 years old bounded down out of the truck, landed in the drift beside the snow-covered Amy and said, "Hello. You look like you could use some help." He was wearing a high school athletic jacket with an "M" on it, a blue stocking cap and a smile bigger than outside. He introduced himself as Kevin Clark and stated that he lived in the next town, Marshall, which was about three miles away.

"I have never been so glad to see another human being in all my life," she said. She then told him how she came to be stranded and that she had no idea where she was.

He said that he decided to drive along the Interstate to see if anyone was stranded and needed help. He offered two options: (1) Break the window and get inside, or (2) He would take her to Marshall where they would try to find a key or a Slim Jim. A Slim Jim is a flat metal device that can be slipped down beside the window to the locking mechanism and open the door.

Amy had to decide if she wanted to break the window or trust Kevin enough to go with him. Instantly thoughts flashed through her mind of the many stories she had heard of women who had been kidnapped, abused and even killed by accepting such offers along the highway. She quickly surveyed her options. She could stand here beside the car and freeze to death. She could have Kevin break the window and then try to drive on home. She could get in the truck with a stranger and hope for the best. He was a friendly young man and she thought he had an honest looking face. Her decision was made.

She climbed up into the truck with an assist from Kevin. Immediately she felt the warmth of the heater on her face. It took several minutes for her body to warm to a comfortable level. The truck moved effortlessly through the snow toward town. Kevin was truly an angel in disguise. He drove to the car dealership in Marshall to find a key. They were trying to close up and go home also and no one could help.

Kevin returned to the truck where Amy was now as warm as a piece of toast. He gave her the bad news. All Amy could think of now was her car sitting under an overpass, engine running, lights on, keys inside, a ripe plum and easy picking for any person who may venture along. Kevin drove down the snow-blown streets to the police department. Two of the policemen knew him. Reluctantly, they gave him a Slim Jim that might possibly open the door.

Kevin and Amy then labored back over the three-mile journey down the blizzard-blown interstate toward her car. They struggled through whiteouts and howling wind. The car was still sitting in the blowing snow with its lights on struggling to keep vigil. Kevin climbed down into the roaring snow, rammed the tool down beside the window, wiggled it a couple of times, pulled upward and the door opened. They both cheered. Amy jumped down from the truck and immediately crawled inside her friendly car.

Kevin then took a snow shovel out of his truck, scooped the snow away from the wheels so she could get started. He then cleaned all of her windows while she sat inside. He gave her a little push and she was able to move into the tracks the truck had made. It was still doubtful that she could make it the next 15 miles to Terre Haute.

Amy thanked him profusely and offered to pay him whatever he asked. He refused her offer. "But," she said, "if you had not come along there is no telling what might have happened to me. I could have died." He replied, "I know, but that is why I am out here today. I came to help anyone who might need it. I did not come out here to make money or take advantage of you. I just want to help. Now if you will follow me, we will try to get you safely into Marshall where you can wait out the storm."

Amy could not believe her good fortune. In her hour of deepest dread and fear, Kevin came along and pulled her from the iron grip of Old Man Winter. At that very moment, another fortuitous event happened. Like an angel of light looming out of the darkness, a huge snowplow hove into sight, blown down the road like a tumbleweed in a dust storm. Sensing her opportunity, Amy again gratefully thanked Kevin, and drove off behind the snowplow. She followed it all the way into Terre Haute, Indiana, and arrived at her apartment at 8:30 pm. Within an hour after she got home, a snow emergency was declared for the entire area, banning all vehicular travel except for emergency vehicles.

The blizzard locked everyone in and shut the community down for a few days. It took two more weeks for all operations to return to normal. What would Amy have done without Kevin? Where would she be today? He truly was a lifesaver. As she left my office, I said, "Now you see why I would worry if my daughter was on the road as you are." She smiled and said, "I know," and went on her way.

Howie: Evel Knievel Wannabe

Howie is a salesman. He is good at it. I have known him for nearly three lustra - remember a lustrum is five years. In that time he has sold RV's, copy machines, coffee, insurance, cars, computers, electronic equipment, timeshare condos and other products too numerous to mention.

One day, about dusk, he finished his last appointment and was traveling around Indinapolis on I-465 on his way home. As usual the traffic was heavy and fast. He was a bit preoccupied and nearly missed his exit. At the very last moment, he swerved, ran along the berm for a short distance, then through the grass, bumped across the concrete safety lane, jumped over the rumble strips, leaped the drainage channel and just made the turn. During that perilous flight he "bottomed out" and did some major league bouncing as he careened along over hill and dale. It never occurred to him to go to the next exit and come back and upon that salient fact hangs this tale.

After a short period of time, his heart beat returned to the vicinity of normal, his breath stopped coming in wheezing gasps and his blood pressure descended to something in the neighborhood of normal. He then became aware of a terrible scraping and grinding noise coming from under the car. He summoned his memory bank of such noises and deduced that he had either lost his muffler or he had knocked his exhaust system off and it was dragging. Listening more closely, he concluded that when he had used the "Dukes of Hazzard" maneuver to make the exit, he must have knocked his exhaust system off. What a racket it made.

Of course it was making a terrible noise. And of course all of the other drivers were looking at him and smirking at his plight. I have had the same experience. I feel self-conscious and embarrassed because it seems that everyone is looking and laughing at, the redneck white trash driving a pile of junk.

Howie was running late and he didn't quite know what to do. He stopped at the next opportunity, looked in the trunk of his car and all he found there was a long extension cord. He saw part of the exhaust system sticking out from under the car. He reached under the car as far as possible and tied the cord around the pipe and muffler. He then passed the cord through the back window, across the seat and out the window on the other side and tied it as securely as possible to the pipe sticking out that side. Going to the other side of the car, he tied the cord to the pipe and secured it to the door handle. He then closed the windows as far as possible to tighten the cord. At that moment he said that he looked like the Clampett family moving to Beverly Hills.

He continued on homeward stopping to pick up his daughter at middle-school. Needless to say his repairs did not completely prevent the dragging pipes, and the cord and suspended rusty exhaust system were more than a little embarrassing. As he clunked to the front of the school his daughter was standing there with a gaggle of her friends. She was mortified at having to get in that wreck with her dad. She got in, slammed the door, slunk down in the seat, made herself invisible and screamed, "Let's get out of here! I am so embarrassed." Howie clanked and clamored his way down the street toward home.

That night he had to go to a sales meeting and he barely had time to get himself and his daughter home, grab a quick dinner and go out again. Needless to say he had to take more grief from people along the way as they laughed, chuckled and pointed at him clamoring down the street. Some of the guys at the sales meeting gave him a hard time accusing him of littering the street, violating the community noise ordinances and noting his lack of personal pride exhibited by driving that "wreck."

He then screeched home and went to bed. The next morning the same embarrassment rode with him on the way to work. He stopped at a muffler shop near his place of employment and explained what had happened and asked the owner to see what he could do to fix the problem. The owner promised to call him to give an estimate on what it would cost to replace the exhaust system or to repair it. He walked the two blocks to work.

Later on that morning, Howie's phone rang. It was Earl at Earl's Muffler Shop. He was chuckling as Howie answered the phone. "What do you think it will cost?" queried Howie. Earl almost laughed and replied, "Oh it is going to cost a lot." Howie ears picked up and he was concerned now. "Don't play with me," he said, "how much do you think it will be?" Earl burst out laughing and said, "Son, you don't need a new tailpipe or exhaust system. When you did that Evel Knievel thing you picked up and old muffler and tail pipe under your car and you've been dragging it around town ever since. You took real good care of it though," he said roaring with laughter. Howie had to laugh too, but not long. He was exhausted.

Rocky Loves To Push The Envelope

Rocky is a mischievous sort. He is young and full of energy. As you may have deduced by now, BW (my wife) and I are not so young and not so full of energy. We are not old or even middle-aged because old and middle-aged people are at least ten years older than you are no matter how old you are.

Rocky is also quite curious. He will: look at and into everything, feel everything, touch everything, taste everything, explore everything and frequently break things he manipulates. He is never where you want him to be and he is always where you do not want him to be. If we want him to zig he will zag. If we want him to zag he will zig. If we want him to be quiet he is noisy and makes sure everyone knows that he is around. If we want him to make noise he is quiet and sneaky.

He has a ravenous, rapacious appetite. It seems that he is always eating or wanting something to eat. To us it appears that as soon as he is finished eating he begins to look for his next meal or snack. I thought I ate a lot until he came along. He eats constantly.

He plunders around through BW's flower garden and even when we have given clear indications and instructions not to get in there, he frequently ignores those directions and tiptoes through the tulips, stomps through the nasturtiums and rollicks through the roses. This is extremely frustrating to us especially BW who strives to keep those flower gardens in a state of perpetual beauty and splendor that would make the groundskeepers at the Palace of Versailles green with envy. It is not difficult to see where he has meandered carelessly through those beautiful blossoms. He is nosy.

You might say that he is very inquisitive. He wants to see how things are and how they look close up. He seems to want to investigate every growing thing. He wants to scrutinize every inanimate thing. So, he will roll it over, pick it up, taste it, chew on it and manipulate it every way possible. How can you be angry at an inquisitive being like that? In fact, curiosity is a very good quality and characteristic if kept in check and used properly. I am not sure Rocky has mastered that yet. I am sure he hasn't.

Curiosity gets the best of him and he will pull the hummingbird feeder down to see how it works and to determine if the liquid in there is actually sweet. What is wrong with that? BW thinks that he should come and ask first. That makes sense to me but Rocky has another world-view.

He enjoys watching birds feed but he also wants to know how the food tastes. He has been known to jump up or reach up and pull on the feeder until it falls to the ground. Most likely the feeder will burst open and spill the seeds. That gives Rocky the opportunity to feel and taste the feed up close and personal. If he would ask we would let him have some and he would not have to plunder and pillage like Hagar the Horrible. He never asks.

There are few people more grouchy than a couple of old cranky, sleepy people who want to rest and can't. You can deprive me of many things and I will excuse you or forgive you. However, you better not get between me and the bedroom when I head for my 'plo' and 'binky'. And, unless you want to feel my number 13's in your callipygian cleft - your backside - you better not get in my way when dinner is ready.

But Rocky has weird sleeping habits. Quite frequently he sleeps during the day and is wide-awake at night. While we are trying to sleep or getting ready to sleep, he is raring to go and is up and at 'em. Therefore, our biorhythms and time clocks are always out of synchronization. That does cause some conflict in our household.

When Rocky destroys the bird feeder or knocks the hummingbird feeder down, BW is livid. She is ready to beat him within an inch or half-inch of his life. When he plunders and blunders through my garage and knocks things off the workbench, I get angry. When he climbs over the shelves or through the cabinets, I get mad. If he breaks something, I become acrimonious. Acrimonious is way beyond mad. It is purple-faced mad. It is madder than a wet hen and you know how mad that is.

"Why does he do that?" BW shrieks in agony and pain when she sees what Rocky has done. Her voice sounds like the roar of a 747 going overhead. I say, "You can't beat him, forget trying to keep bird feeders. You can not win!" "I will not let him win. I am determined to beat him at his game," She retorts! Gentle reader, thus far it is Rocky 835 and BW 0. Does that give you a clue as to who is winning?

The truth is, Rocky will always win. BW must come to grips with that lucid fact. All we can do is barricade the house and garage and hope for the best. Rocky is a raccoon who lives in the woods behind our house.

I Won The Hay Field World Series

A short time ago I was doing an archeological dig through an old out building on the farm North of Calvertville. It is one of those buildings where people store items no longer in use but too good to throw away. It is like a refrigerator. A refrigerator is a place where people keep leftovers until it is time to feed them to the garbage disposal. The items in the building looked like they should have been discarded many moons ago.

It was on that archeological dig that I found the baseball mitt that I had as a child. Dad bought brother and me each a mitt when we were very short in the tooth. It was much smaller than I remembered and it was vintage Ty Cobb. It looked like the mitts that the old time professional players wore in the 1920s and 1930s. The fingers were not sewn together, there was minimal padding and the mitt was not much larger than the hand that it fit. The genuine cowhide leather was mildewed, cracked and dried. A mud dauber had built a condo in it.

That old mitt became a time machine that transported me back to a time and place when brother and I played many a World Series Game of one on one. We didn't have a regular baseball diamond. The only places we could play were in the hay fields just after the hay had been harvested or in the lot out behind the barn. When we lined up to play that field magically became Yankee Stadium or Sportsman Park in St. Louis. Dad was a St. Louis Cardinal fan so naturally we were too. Many a hot summer night we sat outside and listened to KMOX out of St. Louis and pretended that we were playing with Stan Musial, Marty Marian, Red Schoendienst and Enos Slaughter.

My memory took me back to the times that dad played baseball with us. Many times it was just the three of us but we had some hotly contested games. Dad would hit grounders and fly balls to us by the hour even after a long day of work when he must have been tired. I can still see him holding the bat in his right hand in the hitting position, then tossing the ball up with his left hand, and quickly gripping the bat with both hands. He would hit that ball out of sight. The ball would fly around the sun and then come down while brother and I circled like wolves around a stray buffalo. We watched and waited and held our mitts at the ready and finally the ball re-entered the atmosphere trailing a plume of sparks. Sometimes we caught it sometimes we didn't. No one seemed to mind. Then we recycled it to dad who would hit it again. He always seemed to be pondering something as he hit the ball.

A rag, a piece of wood, an old shirt or a feed sack were all pressed into service as bases. It was three guys clad in t-shirts, caps and brogan shoes. Dad would pitch, one of us would play the field and the other would bat. Dad did not need a mitt because his hands were so large. He would take his place at the pitchers mound and go into his windup. He would flail his arm and wind it up like a huge windmill then kick his leg up and throw the ball toward the plate. I would swing like a rusty gate and if I did hit the ball it would be a worm burner or a blooper that barely made it back to him. Sometimes it would go beyond him.

Then I would sling the bat and blast off like a rocket toward first base. Dad would field the ball and the race was on. A benevolent dad would rarely make it in time to tag me out or if he did mysteriously he would drop the ball and yell "Safe." Then I would try to steal second. I did with regularity because we frequently would collide, fall down and dissolve into laughter and I would be safe again. Frequently I would turn a bloop hit into an inside the park homerun by just reaching home a nanosecond before dad or brother arrived with the ball. When dad took his turn at bat, he always made an out at first. He never had the strength to hit the ball past the pitcher even though he was six feet tall and weighed 220 pounds. Isn't that amazing?

31

I was saddened when baseball kicked me in the shins about seven years ago when they canceled the World Series because the pampered players with obscene, bloated salaries and overfed egos wanted even more. Sorry guys, you lost me and I don't miss you. I haven't watched a game since. But I do miss those games when brother, dad and I played in Hay Field Stadium.

We played many a game in the warm summer sun. Brother and I dreamed of becoming big league players while dad was transformed into a kid again. We hated to stop for supper. Ah yes, baseball, the way it should be played between a dad and his sons.

You Gotta' be Smarter Than the Machinery

"You gotta' be smarter than the machinery to make the machinery work," is a saying that I grew up with. In those days when I was much shorter in the tooth, the axiom was uttered as a mild insult because the machinery was much simpler and it didn't take a super level of intelligence to operate it. And now to bring everyone up to speed, an adage for the 21st century is "You gotta' be smarter than the technology to make the technology work." And thereby hangs the tale.

BW and I were making our regular trek to Greene County to visit our mothers. I stopped at the Thornton Station at I-70 and state road 267 in Plainfield, Indiana, to fuel the car and my battle with technology began. A cold drizzling rain greeted me as I heaved myself out of the warm car. Gasoline was 92 cents which made the purchase more endurable. I am caused to wonder about the conundrum that we supposedly live in a service economy when more often the one paying the bill performs the services. Pumping your own gas is a case in point. Bagging your own groceries is another. But I digress.

I inserted my debit card into the slot on the pump, magnetic strip up, using my right hand, and removed it quickly as per the directions. You know the routine. Nothing happened. A message flashed on the small screen and instructed me to insert my card. I repeated the process and waited for authorization. Again the message blurted out, "Please insert your card." For the third time I repeated the routine and received the same irritating message. I smoothed the card like a dollar bill for a pop machine thinking that might work. Nothing. I turned it upside down with the same results. Now the message said, "Hey Dim Bulb, insert your card."

Okay, I thought, I have a Ph.D. and I can't make this stupid pump work. What is the problem? I looked at the diagram again preparing to storm the Bastille and demand satisfaction. Mentally I was prepared to dive bomb my car through their front door and politely ask for assistance.

So there I was, getting madder by the moment, standing in the blustery winter wind with rain spotting my glasses and trickling down my shirt collar. I would have crossed the road to the BP station but gas was $1.12 there. Old Man Winter had his bony cold fingers around my neck and my skinny body was damp and shivering but I leaped into the breach one more time. This time I placed the card in my left hand inserted it with the magnetic strip on top and magically the card was authorized. As the gasoline was flowing into the tank, I looked at the diagram one more time and had an epiphany. I had been inserting the card with the magnetic strip on the wrong side. I felt like I was driving on Dumb Street in Stupidville. You gotta' be smarter than the technology to make the technology work. Duh!

She Did Not Know Captain Kangaroo

I don't know how much more I can take. Lately my self-esteem, self-image and fragile psyche have been bludgeoned into submission by the cudgel of reality. My self-image has been made so small that I could walk fully erect under a snail trail. My psyche has been so diminished that I now can play handball on the curb in front of our house and we don't even have a curb. My self-esteem is as insignificant as a dust bunny under the dresser in the back bedroom beneath the stairs covered by a tarpaulin in the guest house of a long dead Gold Rush shanty in a ghost town in Southern Nevada that was shattered by atomic testing in 1943.

BW and I along with some friends were eating in a restaurant on Indy's West Side. Our server was a friendly, young female. You can't say waitress any more because it is not politically correct. She was wearing an apron that had several large pockets on the front and sides in which she carried bottles of various condiments and ancillary items. It seemed to be quite handy and efficient. I remarked, "You have more pockets in your apron than Captain Kangaroo had in his jacket."

She looked at me and grew puzzled. Her forehead looked like corduroy and she said, "Captain who?"

Well imagine my surprise. My "sixhead", some of us don't have as much hair as we once had, became furrowed and I sank down in my chair, pleading, "Captain Kangaroo. He had a television show for children that ran for nearly thirty years. Mr. Green Jeans, the Bunny Rabbit and the Clock were all on the show."

She smiled benignly and said, "I never heard of him or his show." It quickly became apparent that she was culturally deprived. I could tell just by looking at her. But that is not the end of the story. There is more.

BW and I had a holiday party at our house. We were playing Family Feud. Admittedly it was the first edition but it was manufactured in the late 70s - the 1970s not the 1870s. One question asked for cast names of the huge western TV show Gunsmoke. You know who I am talking about - Matt Dillon, Chester Good, Kitty Russell, Doc Adams, Festus Hagen, Ma Smalley, Moss Grimmick and others. Three people in the group of ten had never heard of Gunsmoke. They had never seen it and knew nothing about it. It gets worse.

BW and I were talking and wondering if Staples might still sell carbon paper. How many people today have used carbon paper? A young office worker of today never uses it and probably has never used a typewriter.

I was getting a rental car at a local repair shop. We have had six accidents since we moved to the metro area. Not one of these incidents was our fault. The young woman who represented Enterprise Rental Cars talked me through the form and asked for my signature. Then she asked that I initial four other places to indicate that she had explained other options or that I had rejected or accepted portions of the deal. I remarked, "This sounds like Radar on M*A*S*H when he had Col. Blake initial that he had signed and signed that he had initialed various army forms. She looked puzzled. I continued, "You know Corporal Radar O'Reilly. The company clerk. He was from Ottuma, Iowa. He was short and wore glasses and slept with a Teddy Bear." I could tell by her lack of expression that she was blissfully unaware of who Radar was.

There were three people in the office at the time - two women who were 20 something and a man who was early 30 something. None of them knew who Radar was or had ever watched the TV show M*A*S*H. I slumped in defeat. There was some vindication later.

When I returned the rental car there were four people in the office area. Three different people and one who was there during the previous conversation. I politely mentioned the conversation about M*A*S*H. This time the three new people had all heard of the show and knew who Radar was. What a relief. I thought I was in the Twilight Zone.

I can just hear someone ask, "What do you mean the Twilight Zone?" That is another column. Move over Methuselah and Rod Serling, I have to sit down.

The Magic of A Laundry Hamper

There is something magical about a clothes hamper. Most men do not appreciate the magic that happens in that vessel. They are unaware because they merely toss their used and dirty clothing on the floor and someone else, translated wife, picks it up and provides proper maintenance for the foul, filthy, fuming, fusty, foaming, fetid fashions.

It pains me to talk to people who have a tremendous grasp of the obvious. Mostly you don't talk to them, they talk and you listen. Therefore, it pains me to say this but MEN AND WOMEN VIEW LAUNDRY DIFFERENTLY. WHAT A REVELATION! What is laundry? Perhaps some definitions are in order. My Webster's Ninth New Collegiate Dictionary defines laundry as clothes or linens that have been or are to be laundered. Launder means to wash in water to make ready for use by washing and ironing. Laundry woman means, well you know what that means.

Back to laundry. Women see clothing in two distinct arenas or piles: Dirty and clean. Men see laundry in several arenas or piles: clean, kind of clean, semi-clean, dirty and fungus growing on them. Kind of clean clothes are easily wearable again and again. Semi-clean clothes are hanging in the closet but not on a hanger. They are available at a moments notice. Dirty clothes can be worn again if needed. Fungus growing on them clothes, are ready for laundry, maybe.

I have noticed that women tend to wear a garment one time and it goes into the laundry hamper, especially underwear. Men tend to wear a garment more than one time before assigning it to the hamper. We do not understand why clothing cannot be worn more than one time, including underwear. Socks, for example must have a crust on them that holds the sock open and ready for inserting the feet before being deemed too dirty. Shirts can be worn, hung on

38

the hook on the closet door, worn again and in case of an emergency or just because I like the shirt, it can go out again perhaps under a jacket. It can be worn but you must remember to keep your arms tightly pressed to your side.

In consideration, jeans can be worn almost indefinitely before washing. They have the ability to ward off dirt and germs and continue to serve. Jeans have the innate ability to resist stains and soil and flake off major things such as catsup, grass stains, grease and oil and still remain presentable.

T-shirts and sweatshirts have the uncanny ability to fend off uncleanness and be available for wearing innumerable times. It is magic. No one can explain it. Near the end, however, the sniff test is required. If you can hold the shirt within an arm's length of your nose and it does not smell like the cow barn at the state fair, it is wearable.

Socks with a hole in them are still usable. You just have to be careful where the hole is placed. If it is in the toe region, extreme care must be exercised when it is put on the foot to keep certain toes, namely the great toe, from protruding through the hole. By the way, who died and named that toe the "Great Toe?" Why is that toe so much greater than the little piggy that cried wee, wee, wee all the way home? How about the little piggy that had roast beef? Doesn't he count? I think so.

If the hole is in the back near the top of your shoe, you must not pull the sock too high or skin will show through. I have known people to use a magic marker to color their skin when wearing black socks with holes in them. How creative! Okay, I did it.

Fungus growing on them clothes, have registered for courses at many universities. Men will keep old broken down tennis shoes with holes in them, broken strings and holes in the soles you can read the paper through. They never go in the laundry. Look in a man's closet and you will find old shorts with rips and slashes in them, with holes and frayed hems, but they are still wearable.

Men look at a pile of laundry and see clothing that can be worn for at least another decade. Women look at a pile of male laundry and see rags to use in washing the car or cleaning the toilet bowl.

You are probably asking yourself right now, what kind of magic occurs in the laundry hamper. The magic occurs when I place a foaming, foul, fetid, fuming, filthy, fusty garment in the laundry hamper and it magically reappears in my closet, on a hanger or in my dresser drawer, clean, pressed, smelling great and ready to wear. Magic. David Copperfield, eat your heart out.

From Paw Paws to Twinkies
I Am Hooked

Ok. I admit it. I am a Twinkaholic. I attend meetings and I am on a 12-step program that I am failing abysmally. I don't care. I really do not have my heart, soul and mind in the program. If so, I would be off them now and in recovery.

I believe that it all began many years ago in Highland Township, Indiana, where I grew up. My father and mother purchased a farm north of Calvertville in 1941 for a few dollars less than $4,000. It was approximately 200 acres with house, barn and other out buildings. I told my dad on several occasions what a deal they got. A bare lot of approximately one acre or less, with no trees, landscaping or house in suburbia where I live costs as much as $30,000. If you add some trees and interesting terrain, it goes as high as $35-40,000. Recently three acres sold near our house for $250,000. "Son," he said, "When we signed our names to that mortgage, I had no idea in this world how I would ever pay it off." But pay it off they did in less than four years. And to my knowledge they never went into debt again. They lived by the axiom, "If you don't have the money, you don't need it."

And now back to the story. It was on that farm that I was introduced to a delectable product of the woods known as a paw paw - the Indiana banana. One day Dad, Brother and I were trekking through the woods when dad reached into the leaves and branches of a rather small tree and pulled out a yellowish brown fruit-like item that looked like a short, rotund banana. He took a bite and then offered us the same. Somewhat reluctantly I squeezed the thick banana like skin of the fruit and there flowed into my mouth an elixir of such delightful essence that I was besotted. The flavor surpassed the vaunted ambrosia of the Greek Gods. At that time, however, I had never heard of ambrosia, but it was 'larapin'. 'Larapin' is an old down home country word that means it is gooooood. I could not get enough of that magic pudding-like fruit. That was the moment that started me down the road to Twinkie Land.

If you get a paw paw at the right time, they are incredibly delicious. The skin is a bit inedible, so the consumer squeezes the delicacy and the insides come flowing out like icing out of the tube. Superb! However, much like a persimmon, if it is not the right time, ugh-a-mundo they are terrible. They never grew in abundance so the scarcity makes them more delightful.

My mom baked the best cakes in the universe. My favorites were white cake and yellow cake. I always licked the batter from the bowl, that is if I could sneak it away from my brother and the Killer - my big mean sister. Mom also made wonderful frostings. We often ate ice cream with cake and often whipped cream and fruit were added. I am drooling just remembering. Those wonderful cakes also contributed to my downward slide into the Kingdom of Twinkie.

Fast forward. Take a look at a little overall clad kid standing in the Calvertville General Store looking at the bread and cookie counter. There nestled among the plastic sheathed delicacies was a new treat called Twinkies. I had never eaten one. They looked like two small paw paws, or two bananas or two yellow torpedoes. The wrapper said there were two sponge cakes with a creamy filling. I had to have one. I ate that Twinkie and my tongue danced a jig that The Lord of the Dance could not imitate. He would be absolutely verdant with envy. My brain told my body that it wanted more of that delectable morsel. "Whatever it takes," said the brain to the body, "I want Twinkies!" And my experience that day propelled me farther down the road to addiction. Today I could eat a bushel basket full of Twinkies before noon.

I read recently of a scientific research project on Twinkies conducted by two college students at Rice University during finals week. Well what would you expect from someone going to a university named after a breakfast cereal and a major ingredient of pilaf.

They found that Twinkies did not know the answers to several questions that humans knew. They also put some Twinkies in a microwave oven and nuked them for 30 seconds after which they imploded and incinerated. They concluded that microwaving a Twinkie is a bad idea.

Next the researchers took some Twinkies to the top of a six-story building and dropped them to the sidewalk. They concluded that gravity affects Twinkies. They shot electricity through a Twinkie and concluded that that was boring. They soaked one in rubbing alcohol and set it on fire and concluded that Twinkies could be a suitable substitute for firewood under certain conditions.

Lastly they placed several Twinkies in a whirring blender for a short period of time and then placed the goo in a test tube. They concluded that Twinkies are 68 percent air and 32 percent Twinkie stuff which allows one to compress 100 of them into a space of 32. That information is pertinent if you are packing to go on a trip.

I plan to share this information at my next support group meeting. In my estimation, though, that was a horrible waste of good Twinkies.

Pass The Gravy Please

I was among a large contingent of people gathered for an evening of celebration. It was a festive occasion to celebrate the holidays. The room was decorated with festive streamers, balloons and other cheerful garlands. The temperature was a little high because the room was overflowing. People were packed in not like sardines but close to it. There was one aisle in the room that had to accommodate all of the movements of the crowd plus the wait staff.

The crowd was a bit boisterous because they were celebrating and in a festive mood. The kitchen staff was understaffed because of mid-winter illnesses. The evening did not get off to a good start.

There was no standard or basic menu. Each person had the opportunity to order and pay for his or her own meal from a list of four entrees. That greatly complicated the ordering, serving and eating process. A further complication was that the kitchen was on the first floor and we were meeting on the second floor.

The wait staff did a remarkable job dodging those going to the rest rooms and those roaming the single aisle to talk to others in the room.

We were to eat at 6:00 but it was 7:15 when the final meals were served. The winded and tense staff with faces glowing from the effort served the final table that was near me. One woman whose face looked as if she had just smelled something she did not like began to complain. She had been served fried chicken, green beans and mashed potatoes with brown gravy. "I ordered white gravy on my potatoes," she groused.

Two or more associates seated near her tried to convince her that she should take the brown gravy and not cause a problem. "It is so late in the evening, they just made a mistake," two of her friends said.

"Made a mistake, you know that I don't like brown gravy!" she whined, her voice sounding like a Skilsaw cutting through aluminum roofing.

"They just got you mixed up with someone else's order."

"I don't care, I will not eat this crap!"

"There isn't much difference in brown and white gravy! Why don't you just eat it and let it go?"

"I will not! They made the mistake and they will have to correct it! I will not put up with their incompetence."

"I'll gladly trade you my food. I haven't touched it yet and my potatoes have white gravy on them," one of the ladies said.

"I will not take your food. Then you will not have what you ordered! That isn't fair and it isn't right, and I'm not going to touch this food until it is right!"

The wait staff was harried and hurried all evening. By the time the last table had been served the main course, they were beginning to clear the other tables and taking dessert orders. They were still dodging the rest room crowd in the aisle. Now those who were finished with the main course were standing to talk to others and some were in the aisle moving around. The offended woman would not be placated. She would not eat. She would not be convinced to accept the meal graciously and enjoy the evening.

"Then why don't you just eat the meat and the green beans and leave the potatoes alone?" one asked.

"I like potatoes but they have to be right," she retorted. "I ordered chicken, green beans and potatoes with white gravy and that is what I expected to get, that is what I was promised, and that is what I demand and I am not going to accept anything less. I won't eat it, I won't touch it, and I won't pay for it either. Little girl, little girl come here."

She snapped her fingers and her mouth at one of the wait staff saying, "Little girl, little girl, come here." One of the wait staff asked, "May I help you?"

"Yes, you may," the lady barked, "You got my order wrong and I want it right. Take this food back and bring me what I ordered."

"What is wrong with the order," asked the server in a concerned and professional manner.

"You put brown gravy on my potatoes and I clearly ordered white gravy!" she snapped.

"I'm sorry, I will bring you a serving of potatoes with white gravy," she replied calmly and quietly, "Just go ahead and eat the other items and I will bring the potatoes in just a moment."

"No," the woman barked louder, "I want you to take this plate of food back to the kitchen and bring me what I ordered now or I want to see the manager."

"That sounds like a reasonable solution," stated one of her embarrassed friends.

"No it isn't," she shrieked with a voice that sounded like a cat impaled on a spear, "I want what I ordered. I will not condone incompetence and slovenly service from these minimum wage lackeys."

By now several people were watching. They were aghast with what was going on. They could not believe how intractable the woman was. They could not believe what she was saying.

The server graciously took the plate back to the kitchen and returned in a few moments with fried chicken, green beans and potatoes with white gravy. The woman did not recognize her and did not thank her. Her associates continued to eat but they were looking intently at their plates and all conversation had ceased. To further demonstrate her utter contempt for the wait staff and the restaurant, the woman refused to eat any of the food. It might have been a good thing, because there might have been some foreign matter in the potatoes. I'll bet she refused to pay also.

It is Payback Time!

It is payback time. It is now my turn at bat, my turn in the limelight, my time for the leading role, no more second banana for me. No more second fiddle playing or waiting in the wings for my cue. For years I have stood in the background and smiled while others took the preeminence and received all the adulation and the glory. I sat on the bench while others played and received attention from the crowd.

While others were telling and retelling their stories of accomplishments and of acclaim for deeds done, I stood meekly by offering kudos and applause. Trophies were displayed and documents of acclaim and awards have been shown and proudly chronicled in my presence while I had nothing to rebut or to countermand such accomplishments.

Multitudes of people have proudly displayed a myriad of pictures to document beauty as well as moments of idolization accorded themselves and those with whom they associate. There was nothing in my arsenal of scrapbooks or portfolio to demonstrate such inducements for my life. The people I have been referring to are not mean spirited or overbearing. Well some are overbearing. And I mean that in the nicest way possible.

By now you are wondering what the old geezer is blathering about. BW and I are grandparents for the first time. Little, and I mean diminutive, Audrey, which means strong one, was born on June 14 to TM and Todd in New Albany, Indiana. Actually she was born in Norton Hospital in Louisville, Kentucky. I surely hope that doesn't make her a Kentucky Wildcat fan or a Kentuckian by the mere fact that she was born across the river. I do not intend to offend those fine Americans who live South of the Ohio, but Audrey is a Hoosier through and through.

One aspect I know about week old Audrey is that she is unaware of calendars, timelines and the plans of others. It seems that her parents, medical personnel and significant others in her life had the bizarre idea that she was to be born in August. Call me crazy, Miss Scarlet, but those of us who have lived a little longer than she has know about birthing babies. However, Audrey, being the imaginative and assertive sort decided that she had waited long enough and made her own calendar. TM reported that the little tasker had been doing cartwheels, jumping jacks and the Russian Saber Dance for some time. Todd reported that she had kicked at him while he was trying to sleep. So last Thursday morning she yelled "Surprise" and made her appearance.

And now in the pink corner, weighing in at a ponderous two pounds three ounces, Audrey Grace "I'll have you wrapped around my finger in no time" Carter, arrived about two and one half months early. Who does she think she is? Knowing women as I do, that is probably the last time she will be early let alone on time. I am happy and thankful to report that she is not exhibiting any medical problems. Momma was released on Saturday and daddy is recovering. Grandma is still flying higher than the Hubble Telescope.

Child psychologists unequivocally state that it takes time for a child to bond with their parents and grandparents. I can testify that that is true in the case of my own two children and now Audrey. It was truly a moment of magic when I was allowed to go in with TM to see Audrey. She looked like a doll snuggled up in her isolette unit. I reached in and touched her tiny arm and hand. At that moment I detected something, a slight movement in the area of her heart. That something moved up to her shoulder and down her arm and entered my finger. Like an electrical charge it came up my arm to my shoulder and down into my chest and attached itself to my heart. It felt like a tendril from a honeysuckle vine that moved from her heart and wrapped itself around my heart and wouldn't let go. It was hard to see for a moment. As in the case of my daughters, that process of bonding took about one millionth of a nanosecond.

This is a warning! If you see me coming, brace yourself. I will be playing catch up. My sister is a great grandmother. How old must you be to have that title? Don't tell her I told you. My brother has been a grandfather for at least 17 years. And now I have been a grandfather for a week. Prepare yourself to watch slide shows, videotapes and to fawn over massive quantities of pictures. Hone your patience because you will be subjected to endless stories of how pretty Audrey is and how intelligent she is and how progressive she is and how advanced she is ad nauseum.

Stand back world! Give me my due. Prime yourselves for an onslaught from my storehouse of pent up braggadocio. If you would like to contribute some "nappies", send them to Audrey at my address.

Audrey Means The Strong One

Imagine a human being that weighs only two pounds and three ounces? Imagine that same person losing four or five ounces? Now imagine that person a few weeks later who now weighs a corpulent six pounds? If you had tripled your weight in less than three months medical schools around the world would be studying you.

Such a person is Audrey our preemie granddaughter. She is still a small person, but as small as she is she has a huge heart. She has taken six great grandparents, four grandparents, two parents and aunts and uncles and a myriad of other friends into her heart with room to spare.

Sometimes I watch the strong man competition on ESPN. That will indicate how desperate I am for entertainment at times and the depths to which TV goes to fill time. Those men pull huge trucks and airplanes, lift huge stones and carry tree trunks. The typical competitor is six feet five inches tall and weighs over 300 pounds. They are huge and very strong!

Those bruisers have nothing on our Cutie Patootie — Audrey. Did I say Audrey is strong? She is the strongest person I know. She has the strongest fingers I have ever seen. They look small but those fingers are so large that she has wrapped her parents and grandparents around those spindly looking appendages with room to spare. When she yanks those fingers she gets results. She has the strength to carry all of us at the same time.

Audrey has small arms. They appear to be small and frail but she can lift the hearts and spirits of everyone she encounters. She has the ability to cause much work to be done with great speed and all of it is centered on her. Does that sound like a weak person?

Audrey has already developed leadership skills to a level that most adults never attain. She is sagacious enough to supervise a staff of two full-time and four part-time people who provide services for her in: laundry, food service, transportation, medical services, maintenance and housekeeping services, security, night-time supervision, butler and concierge activities, secretarial and communication services plus buildings and grounds and personal hygiene.

A leader and manager must have a commanding and authoritative voice. Law enforcement officers, military commanders, parents and high school principals must have voices that command attention and indicate authority. Audrey has such a voice. She gets work done by suggesting that it be done in a voice that cannot be ignored. Sometimes there is a sense of urgency in the tone and the sound is a bit demanding, nevertheless she gets results and no one questions her position of authority and command.

She is so important that by just existing she commands that her every movement and activity be documented by photographers, videographers and chroniclers of the times.

She also gives new meaning to the term blowout! Blowout on a car tire? Forget about it! Blowout sale at the appliance store? Forget about it! Blowout in a nappie! Now that is a blowout. If you don't know what I am talking about here, stop reading and ask any parent of a preemie or any baby what that means.

Audrey demonstrates a clear understanding of Machiavellian principles because she has no sensitivity to how others feel. She demands attention and services when she wants them. She manipulates others to satisfy her own needs at any time and any place. Language is no barrier to communication with her. She can make other people change by just grunting or crying out in a plaintive voice. I use the word change here with purpose if you know what I mean.

She is a great musician because she plays on everyone's heartstrings. She could be an athletic coach or drill sergeant because at her command people jump and run until they drop. People would run through brick walls to satisfy her every whim and whimsy. She is a human remote control because she controls the volume of the TV and CD player from wherever she is.

She has already learned some feminine wiles because she is playful and cloying. She bats her eyes and others smile and say dumb things. She opens and closes her eyes and commands attention. A simple squeeze from her tiny fingers causes people to melt and giggle like a gaggle of geese. Did I say Audrey is Strong?

A Conversation Between Audrey Grace and her Grampa Van

On the evening of September 27, 2001, Todd and Sharla went out on a date and Grammie and Grampa Van were blessed to spend the evening babysitting with Audrey Grace a.k.a. as CP - Cutie Patootie. During the evening Audrey and I spent some time conversing. I must serve as the interpreter for CP since most of her communication is in "Gruntalian", an obscure language known by only a few people. Luckily I am a linguist of such distinction.

Grampa V. "Hi little CP. Holding you takes me back nearly eight lustrums when your grammie and I were taking care of your Aunt TW when she was your size. And then your mommy, TM, came to live with us a little later. We loved both of them, then and now. They weighed as much at birth as you do after three and a half months. By the way, do you know what a calendar is?"

CP - "No. Tell me, what is a calendar thingy?"

GV - "Well, my little surprise package. It is a way to keep track of time and to set dates when things are going to happen."

CP - "So, what does that have to do with me?"

GV - "Humans like to keep time and schedule events such as when babies are to be born. According to the doctor you should just be two weeks old now. However, you decided to surprise us and come into the world two and one half months ago. You were so small that you gave us quite a scare."

CP - "I like surprises, besides I was crowded. I didn't have enough room to do handstands and to jump around. One night I even kicked daddy. I didn't try to hurt him it was just my way to remind him that I was there. **I am Audrey, hear me roar.**"

GV - "He must have been surprised."

CP - "He did jump back a little ways. It made him chuckle. I loved it. I had to giggle too."

GV - "Well you did arrive after a couple of days of indecision. How did you like Norton Hospital?"

CP - "I loved it there. Everything I needed was supplied without me asking. Even though they were tired, Mommy and Daddy came to see me every day, most days two or three times. They talked to me and sang to me. I can still feel them touching me in the isolette. That felt sooooo good. I felt so loved from the beginning. I didn't mean to scare everybody, I was just tired of waiting."

GV: "One of the things you will have to learn is that sometimes in life you must wait."

CP - "Oh, I don't know if I like that or not! I do know that I like it when my daddy holds me. His cologne smells so nice. I love it when he holds me in his arms and talks to me. I love his nice quiet voice. He is so patient. It must come from his work. Get it? A little dental humor there, Grampa. He always talks about my sweet cheeks."

GV - "So what about your sweet cheeks?"

CP - "I must have sweet cheeks because both of them talk about my cheeks when they change my nappy."

GV - "No, no not those cheeks. They are talking about the cheeks on your face."

CP - "Oh, yeah, [giggles a'plenty]. I do have my mommies cheeks, don't you think? Have you ever seen any cuter cheeks on anyone else, Grampa?"

GV - "Well, maybe once or twice. Maybe as cute but not cuter. What do you think about fishing and playing tennis? Your daddy likes to do both. How do you feel about worms and rackets?"

CP - "I know my daddy likes to play tennis. Have you noticed that I'm always flexing my hands and waving my arms? I am building my strength and one day I'll be able to grip a tennis racket and then I'll beat him. And, he won't have to let me either. By that time he will be so old I'll pass him down the line and lob over his head and bring him to the net and run his legs off. But I'm not so sure about worms and fishing. Mommy doesn't like worms and I don't either. It's a girl thing, you know."

GV - "You know your mommy and daddy love you very much. And your grammies and grampas also love you."

CP - "I know. My mommy doesn't eat things that could hurt my tummy even though she really likes them. Even before I was born she remembered and ate only good things for me."

GV - "Grammie Van is crazy about you. She carries your picture everywhere and brags about how cute you are and how smart and progressive you are. She is as proud of you as she was with your mommy and aunt TW."

CP - "She only says those things because they are true. She is so easy — a real softy. I have already found out that I can get anything I want from her. I just grunt, squawk or cry and she is on it. It is hard not to giggle. I almost laugh out loud. You think that crazy crooked grin is gas, think again, pilgrim, it's just me suppressing a giggle."

GV - "Are you aware that you keep your mommy and daddy up at night and they miss a lot of sleep."

CP - "I know and I don't mean to. It's just that I get gas and my tummy hurts. I just have to scrunch up and move around some. And then I get hungry."

GV - "That is why I also call you WB for wiggle britches."

CP - "Real funny, Grampa. You might think that I have the world figured out, but I don't. I really feel uncertain sometimes. Being born is all so new to me. Maybe I should have waited a while longer. But I feel so good when Mommy and Daddy hold me. I couldn't stand it if they didn't. I sure feel good nestled next to my mommy. I can feel her breath on my face and I know she is near, and I hear her heart beating just like before I was born. When her arms are wrapped around me I feel like a part of her again. She talks to me with her loving voice and tells me she loves me. That makes me feel soooo good. I know that I can make it through the night when she holds me close."

GV: "Aren't mommies wonderful? That is what they do best."

CP - "Grampa. I'm getting sleepy. May I have another milk snack before I nod off? I'm feeling a bit hungry. Oh, and by the way, I feel something unpleasant in my nappy. Would somebody take care of that too?"

GV - "I think Grammie, the easy one, can arrange both of those items for you. Oh, softy, I mean Grammie."

CP - "Slurp, slurp, smack, smack. Burp. ZZZZZZZZZZZZ."

Working in a Jack Factory Can Be An Uplifting Experience

Stanley was an intelligent boy. He had a pleasant personality and most people liked him. He had a kind attitude and generous heart and he liked people. Some would say that he was a people person. A cliché but true. He had a very successful school career in elementary and secondary schools. He made good grades, he was well liked and he had a positive experience. After high school, though, he didn't know what he wanted to do with his life. For a time he was at loose ends and couldn't get the ends tied together.

For a year or so, he knocked around with various jobs from burger flipper, to convenience store worker, to temporary roofer, to lawn maintenance and landscaping. He was a good worker and his employers had positive comments about his work ethic and the way he got along with other employees. He pulled his own weight and frequently the weight of others. None of these jobs lasted more than a season or two and he found himself floundering. He looked into the future and did not like what he saw. However, he thought that he was not prepared to do much else. He felt like the person who invented 6^{up}.

One evening after he had worked all day on a roofing job, he was quite tired and sun burned. His back and legs were sore from all of the lifting, bending and hammering. After showering and eating dinner, he sat down to relax and read the newspaper. He did not usually read the classified ads, but on this day he did and fortuity struck his life.

The ad that caught his eye was from a small factory in the area near his home. The ad said that they were seeking hourly employees. He thought that he might apply because the job offered more stability than his present work and it was inside both winter and summer. That aspect had a measure of appeal to him. He decided to apply for a job and that decision changed his life forever as well as the life of Nathan.

It was a small business that only employed about 25 people and some of them were part-time. They made jacks. They were not car jacks but a kind of all-purpose jack that would be used by farmers, builders, construction workers and others who periodically needed to lift heavy objects. He went to the factory the next day and applied. They liked his attitude, his educational background and the good report from his references and former employers. He was offered a job and he went to work the next Monday.

The job paid more than he was used to making but not enough to retire on. However, the job was steady and had some meager insurance benefits. It did not take Stanley very long to become proficient in his job on the assembly line. Within a short time, he was a well-oiled machine himself as he quickly and deftly completed his tasks in the assembly process. The job also quickly became repetitious, redundant and mundane.

Nathan was a man a few years older than Stanley was who also worked on the line. He was in his late twenties and had been working there for a few years. They became acquainted and bantered back and forth as guys do. Their breaks and lunch hour were at the same time so they would talk about current events and life in general. Frequently Stanley would discuss items that he read in the newspaper or from other sources. Nathan did not appear to be interested or would make neutral or casual off-handed remarks about them. Stanley noticed that Nathan never read the paper or any of the magazines that were in the break room.

One day Nathan embarrassingly revealed that he could neither read nor write. His family never emphasized education in the hill country where he was raised. When he was quite young he quit school because he just couldn't get the hang of it.

"Do you want to learn to read and write?" Stanley asked, "If you do I will gladly help you in any way I can." Nathan said, "I can't read. I am too dumb. Don't bother. All I can do is put these jacks together." "Just remember what I said if you change your mind," Stanley added.

Nothing more was said about the subject until about a month later, when out of the blue Nathan said, "Were you serious about that reading thing?" Stanley said, "I was as serious as a heart attack." "What can you do?" Nathan asked. "You let me think about it a day or two and we will get started."

Stanley visited with some of the elementary teachers who had taught him to read and asked for suggestions. They gave him several books and other materials to use. Two days later Stanley began to teach Nathan to read and write. Every break and lunch hour were consumed by their work together. They worked together for nearly a year. Nathan loved to come to work because he was learning. Stanley felt alive because the work with Nathan made up for the mundane repetitive work he was doing. He enjoyed coming to work.

Nathan finally could read. He read well enough to take the driver's test to get his driver's license, something that had eluded him for nearly 15 years. He felt positively radiant. Then he thought if I could do this why not something higher and better. He asked Stanley how he might get his high school diploma. They visited with the director of the local vocational school where students prepared to take the GED test. He was directed to a new program that allowed students to work with instructors at their own pace to get their diploma.

Nathan leaped into that opportunity with both feet running. It was slow going at first but as time passed he picked up speed and he became a model student and people began to notice his work and attitude. Stanley continued to help him. His attitude about life changed. He was a new man. In less than 24 months he had completed all of his high school requirements and because of the new program he was granted a high school diploma from the local high school and he was allowed to participate in the regular graduation ceremonies. When his name was announced every graduating student stood, applauded and cheered with great enthusiasm. The faculty cheered. The audience also stood and thunderous applause reverberated throughout the gymnasium. Nathan's face was radiant. His smile was bigger than all outside. His face was wet with tears. He was a graduate, a thirty-something high school graduate.

He continued to work making jacks. After a few days he began to think of his future again. He thought, if I can do this why can't I do more? He applied for entrance to a trade school and at the age of 33, he graduated with honors from the electrician program. He served an apprenticeship and soon was working as an electrician making more money than he ever dreamed he could make. He and his wife bought a house and moved in with their two precious children.

One day the state superintendent of public instruction in conjunction with the governor's task force on education, decided to seek out and honor people who could serve as role models for their vocational programs and to encourage drop-outs to "get their diploma." They did not have to look very far to find Nathan. He was selected to receive recognition and to make a speech at the conference.

On the speakers platform that day was the governor, state superintendent of public instruction, the head of the vocational program in the state, and others. Nathan was introduced to polite applause. He told his story and had people beaming with pride and they applauded loudly. Then he introduced his mother and father and his wife and two children. The crowd applauded again.

Then he said, "There is another person in this audience who is special. He is not sitting on the stage but he should be. Without him, I would still be making jacks and little more than minimum wage. I would still be spending my time in taverns drinking and smoking away my pay. But this man looked beyond my illiteracy and saw something inside me. He saw me as a person and he saw the potential that I had. He is responsible for me standing here today. I don't mean to say that the governor, the superintendent and others are not important, but this man was there for me when no one else was. He saw me drowning in a sea of ignorance and threw me a lifeline. He gave me years of his life and taught me to read and write and inspired me to do better. He lit a fire in me that could not be put out. Ladies and gentlemen let me introduce Mr. Stanley Blanchard."

The applause was deafening. Everyone stood in tribute. There was not a dry eye in the house. Nathan brought Stanley up on the speaker's platform and hugged him so tightly that he could hardly breathe. They both shed tears of joy. The head of the state vocational program gave Stanley his seat and then he sat in the audience for the remainder of the program.

Stanley had changed too. While working with Nathan, he found that he liked helping others and that he loved teaching. He also went to school and a year earlier he had received his bachelors' degree in elementary education. He is now a teacher who is working on his masters' degree and is changing the world one person at a time. Stanley and Nathan are different today. All because one day Stanley noticed an ad in the paper wanting people to make jacks.

Butchering in the Old Days

"We're gonna butcher on Wednesday," Dad would announce. That announcement caused a flurry of activity over the next several days. Butchering day on the farm was the time when we prepared meat for eating and for long term storage. Thankfully our part of the country received electrical power when I was a bit short in the tooth so my memories of meat preservation center on freezing and curing and not the filling of jars with meat and then encasing them with grease.

The weather always created excitement and some wariness. It was always cold and blustery. Frequently snow flurries powdered the landscape and caught in our eyelashes as we worked. People waited for a cold day to do the butchering because it is a hot, smelly, messy, difficult job that is mostly outside work. A roaring fire was started early in the morning because butchering hogs requires many gallons of very hot water. That fire was stoked under a hogshead barrel, how appropriate, to expedite the process. Another fire was needed later to render the lard. Butchering required much wood, water and manual labor. A cold day also helped keep the meat from spoiling in the process. Americans do not know what goes on to get their meat to the table.

Very few people today are familiar with the process of changing a living breathing hog into ham, bacon, tenderloin and sausage. Americans of the 21st Century believe that meat is magically placed in the brightly lit antiseptically clean behemoth grocery stores of today by Porko, Breakfast God to the World. When they eat at Bob Evans, purveyor of cholesterol to the world, all they see is the finished product. The unfinished product comes from a truck or the cooler in the back by the kitchen. I wonder if Bob receives a kickback from the drug magnates who produce Lipitor and all of those other cholesterol lowering drugs.

We would help dad start the fires from wood we had prepared in the preceding days. We got the huge cast iron black kettle out of storage and scoured it until it shone. The barrel was set in place, filled with water and a fire started under it. Knives were sharpened on the whetstone or the sandstone grinder. Saw horses were set up and rough hewn lumber was placed on them for tables. Oilcloth was placed on the tables for cleanliness.

Neighbors would come to help, as we would then go help them. When the water was scalding hot in the barrel, the hog of honor was lead into position. Now for those a bit subject to queasiness read on with trepidation. A well-placed rifle shot ended the hog's life. Immediately the hog's head was removed to let it bleed and prepare for scalding. The hind legs were trussed together and the hog was lifted off the ground with the head down to expedite the bleeding process.

Then Porky Pig was lowered into the barrel of boiling water and allowed to remain there for a period of time. That was done to soften the hair for removal. Then a very sharp large butcher knife was used to scrape the hair off to enhance sanitation and to make the butchering process easier. Besides who would want to eat a pork chop with hair on it. When that was completed the carcass was opened and all of the innards were taken out. Friends if you have not had the privilege of smelling such odoriferous emanations, you have missed one of life's joys. Not really. It stank.

Next came the dissection. The carcass was segmented into quarters and other parts. It was then placed on the large tables where dad and the other adults began the long laborious task of cutting it into pieces.

One of my favorite places on the farm was the smokehouse. We did not smoke any meat but the name was a carry over from the past when people did. The hams, jowl, belly and some shoulder meat were taken to the smokehouse where we rubbed it with Morton's Curing Salt. It smelled wonderful. The salt drew the moisture out of the meat and flavored it. The meat would then be hung from the ceiling until we used it.

Sausage was made from all of the fat and scrap meat that was caused in the process. It was cut into small pieces, mixed with seasonings and then run through the hand powered grinder. We stored it in about two pound packages in the freezer. It probably had about ten thousand grams of cholesterol and fat in each bite, but it was gooooood.

The scraps of fat and huge blobs of fat were tossed into the kettle and melted into lard. The liquid lard was dipped out, strained through cheesecloth and stored in lard cans. The last step in that process was to put the bits of meat and skin into the press to render the last bit of lard. Then we ate the cracklins. They were delicious but also very unhealthy. We didn't know it then.

At the end of a very long and tiring day, after all of the hog had been processed and the equipment put away, we ate the first offering from Sir Hog. We always had fresh tenderloin for supper on butchering day. I can still taste it.

Butchering day was excitement and exhaustion in one full and long day. I wish I could go back and relive those days again. Maybe not. It sure is easy to go to Kroger.

I Thought You Would Never Ask

Chad loved Amy. She didn't know it, but he did. She was outgoing, vivacious and drop dead gorgeous and a townie. He was a nice looking farm kid with curly black hair, a bit shy; everyone liked him. He worked hard before and after school and during the summer because the farm did not allow much time to "briggle butt" around as his dad called it. They had crops, animals and pasture to cultivate. The farm consumed their lives. There were few holidays.

Chad and Amy were classmates. They chummed around in the same crowd through school. They were constantly thrown together in school events. They talked all the time but it was always as friends. He so much wanted their relationship to grow but he didn't know how to make it happen.

Amy was very popular, friendly, outgoing and never wanted for a date or attention. Her eyes were deep pools of azure blue. Many a lovesick adolescent drowned in those pools. They would dive in without a life preserver in a vain attempt to go out with her. Many had to be given CPR after a brief encounter with Amy. Alas and alack, they all were just footnotes in her book of love.

Amy's hair was a cascade of golden sunlit silk that dazzled the guys and made the girls long for blonde hair. Her eyes twinkled like stars in the summer night. Her smile was as big as outside. She had more curves than the Blue Ridge Parkway. She had a personality that instantly made friends and put people at ease. Every guy in the county wanted to date her. She teased and tantalized them simultaneously and kept them off balance and confused. She played them like a three-stringed fiddle.

Chad noticed that she dated many boys but not for very long. She and Chad talked freely about dating and how she couldn't quite find the right guy. And then she would chuckle and demurely say, "How about you, Chad?" He didn't know if she was serious or not so he would just laugh with her not knowing what to say. She gave him signals that she was interested and then when he approached her she would send another signal not to get too close too soon. Chad knew that she could have anyone she wanted and he was keenly aware that he was not the biggest fish on the stringer. He spent many hours driving through the State of Confusion.

They remained friends. Night followed day, day followed night, months and years passed and before Chad realized it, graduation day arrived. She went to Indiana University where she was immersed in college life. Upon graduation she began her career in banking in Indianapolis. Chad graduated from Purdue University in agriculture management. He was hired by a huge agri-business firm and began to work almost immediately. His job took him out of the state for long periods of time and required many hours by himself in hotel rooms. He longed to know what Amy was doing and how she was. The muted feet of loneliness frequently walked through his heart. He would visit his parents infrequently and on some of those occasions he saw her in town and they waved to each other and chatted briefly.

A couple of years later Chad went to the homecoming football game hoping that she might be there. He visited with some of his classmates and furtively looked but did not see her. The game proceeded but it held little interest for him. At halftime he went to the refreshment stand for a coke and hot dog. He looked up and there she was, floating in on a cloud of blond hair and her famous expansive smile. She saw Chad and immediately came over and hugged him. She smelled great. Chad thought the hug was a little more than friendly but he couldn't be sure. They talked for a few moments.

She floated away on a cloud of conversation. After the game the festivities continued in the school cafeteria. She sought him out and purposely steered him to a more secluded spot, nailed him to the wall with her indigo eyes, and demurely asked, "How are you, Chad? Tell me all about what you have been doing with your life?" The essence of her perfume made his knees weak. Her delicate hand touched his face and rested on his arm. Suddenly there was no one else in the room. The whole world narrowed down to just the two of them.

He talked briefly about his job and the company and that he was still unattached. He said that his dad was considering retirement and might turn the farm operation over to him. She said she was in banking and likewise single. They engaged in more small talk. His anticipation skyrocketed through the roof and circled the harvest moon.

Then the question came like a thunderbolt out of the depths of those blue eyes and struck him between the eyes like David's rock struck Goliath. "Chad," she said, "didn't you know that I was crazy about you in high school?" His heart raced, his sweaty hands trembled.

"No," Chad self-consciously mumbled, "you could have had anyone you wanted and you never lacked for dates. I was just a country bumpkin; a nobody; just a friend. I knew that I didn't have a chance with you."

He tried to glance beyond her but once again those baby blues impaled him and she said, "I sent you signals that I was interested. I dated but I waited on you. I spent many a night in the lobby of the Hotel Expectation but never got a room."

Chad could hardly breathe. His heart skipped several beats. He coughed and cleared his throat. Emboldened by her approach, he heard himself say, "Well, Miss Amy Allison Hall, the evening is still quite young. Would you go out with me?"

Her eyes glistened, she touched his cheek, placed her arm in his, put her head on his shoulder and murmured,

"Well, Chadburne Clark Dunn, I thought you would never ask."

It is Graduation Time Again

Music takes me to places I have been and to where I want to go. It casts a spell on me that few other experiences can produce. It can mesmerize, tantalize and hypnotize my mind in ways that cause my emotions to flow like rivers of dreams through the landscape of my life. Wow! Is that profound?

As I write this piece I am sitting at my desk listening to classical music. When I enrolled at Indiana State Teachers College in the fall of, well in the last century, I had to take a class in music appreciation. I was a country bumpkin off a Southern Indiana farm more attuned to Webb Pierce, Hank Snow and Eddie Arnold than Brahms, Bach and Beethoven. How I dreaded the class. However, much to my great surprise, I became addicted to classical music.

I am listening to Pomp and Circumstances March No. 1, written by Elgar. It is on a CD titled Stars and Stripes Forever & the Greatest Marches played by Arthur Fiedler and the Boston Pops Orchestra. If you don't think you are familiar with this piece, it is probably the music you marched into the gymnasium for high school graduation. In a similar vein, some of you don't know the William Tell Overture but mention the Lone Ranger Theme and the lights come on. We played many of these marches in the Rambler Band.

As I listen to Elgar, I am taken back through the rivers of time to May 1956, when Earlene, Leahbelle, Paula, Howard, Harold, Ronnie, Arkie and I sat together in the Worthington gymnasium in our caps and gowns and played with the Mighty Rambler Band for the final time. Nearly half of the senior class that year was in the band. Not a bad percentage. We didn't play Pomp and Circumstances as we were marching, but we did play two other pieces. We wore the heat and humidity like a wool shirt in the haymow in August. Our mothers, aunts and grandmothers were squeezed together in the bleachers wearing their print dresses smelling faintly of lavender. They smiled proudly and bravely as they fanned themselves with funeral home fans, handkerchiefs or whatever was available. Our dads, uncles and grandfathers were working men with faces tanned by toil in the sun and soil. Unaccustomed to wearing suits and ties, they sat there sweating like mules eating Jalapeno peppers.

The ceremony was dignified, solemn and majestic. Superintendent "Doc" Franklin and principal, "Wheezer" Richeson made appropriate remarks. Four class members, including me, made speeches. Diplomas were given. That is a far cry from today.

Beach ball tossing, short shorts, tank tops, flip-flops and tube tops characterize graduation ceremonies today. The audience yells brazenly, sounds air horns, whistles and parades in and out while eating a bucket of chicken. It would not surprise me to see women in thong bikinis at graduation this year. But I go on.

With that dignified service and family support we were launched into the orbit of life. Earlene and Arkie, my brother and sister-in-law and Paula are retired public educators. Howard farms and runs the mill. Ronnie is in sales in Indy and Harold is in the sheep business in Colorado. Leahbelle and her Lt. Col. (ret.) husband live in Kentucky. I retired from public education and became a university professor. We are grandparents and some great grandparents. The river of time flows on. See what music can do to you?

The Wood Burning Stove Did it All

I think that the kitchen is the nerve center of a household. I have many pleasant memories of my mother's kitchen when I was growing up. She spent much of her day in the kitchen preparing meals and cleaning afterward. Even today we spend quite a bit of time doing the same thing. Friends tend to cluster in the kitchen during holidays and other celebrations.

Our kitchen in metro-Calvertville was a place where the family gathered three times each day and ate hearty meals. If there were not five people around the table it meant that someone was ill or dad was working a second job off the farm. When I was very short in the tooth, our kitchen was a sparsely furnished room in the back of the house. There were some cabinets and a countertop and sink with no running water and a table and chairs on one end with a walk-in pantry that housed the cream separator. There were two doorways one into the dining room and one to the outside. Beside the outside door was another small sink with a medicine cabinet on the wall. Beside the small sink was a huge wood burning warm morning kitchen range. It had a stovepipe that rose up about a meter and then turned 90 degrees into the chimney. That wood burning stove did it all.

Mom's range had a black iron top with four lids that could be lifted out to access the firebox. The lazy "S" shaped tool was specially made to fit in a recess in the lid to lift it. On the back of the stove were two shelves. One was open and the other had a door that moved up and down similar to a garage door of today. They were used to store food items and keep them warm.

There were two doors on the front of the stove. One was to the firebox where wood and coal could be put into the grate. On the end of the grate was a place to attach the tool to shake the grate and let the ashes fall down into the ash pan. Of course the ash pan had to be emptied every day and wood had to be brought in. The other door was the oven. The doors and the front were covered with an enameled covering that made it look nice. That stove did it all.

The stove would boil, bake, fry and roast and serve as a hot pad to keep food warm. Mom prepared thousands of great meals on that stove. She would put milk on the back of the stove where it would fester and curdle and eventually become cottage cheese. Bread dough had a permanent parking place on the stove. The stove heated the flat irons. We did not have electricity or gas on the farm or microwave ovens. Gadzooks! How did we survive?

A water reservoir with an enamel coated lid, was on the far right side where mom heated water. It would hold a gallon or two and it would get hot enough to scald a chicken. In the morning dad would get his shaving water out of it. We also kept a teakettle on top of the stove. It would become so crusted with lime that it weighed more than Orson Wells. Our water was harder than a banker's heart during the depression. On wash day the copper boiler was placed on top of the stove to heat laundry water.

It was also a human warmer. I remember bursting into the house as cold as a polar bear's nose and standing close to the stove to get warm. Wet gloves and hats were placed on and in the stove to dry. We would open the oven door and place our stocking covered frigid feet on it to warm them. It also was supplemental heat for the rest of the house. Long after we got electricity mom kept the stove because it kept the kitchen warm.

The stove was an integral part of our health plan. When I got a bad cold, I don't remember ever having a good cold, the stove came to the rescue again. Just before I went to bed, dad would slather Vicks Salve on my neck. Then he would wrap a towel or cloth around the stove pipe until it was one nanosecond from bursting into flame and then swathe it around my neck and whisk me off to bed. I can still feel the hot cloth and smell the Vicks.

Last night the temperature got down to single digits at our house. This morning I wish that I could stand beside mom's stove and get warm and then reach in the oven and get a fresh baked biscuit.

We're Going To Crash!

Robbie drove his "Tank" to school most days. Several high school students drove "Tanks" because it was a fad, the thing to do. A "Tank" is a huge car circa 1960s and 1970s. They were huge cars, boats, that lumbered down the highway. The cars were big, bent and old and had rust mosaics on them, but they were cool. Robbie lived 10 miles out in the country and the "Tank" was his only means to get to school and to get home after activities. He made enough money at his weekend and summer jobs to purchase and maintain his "chick mobile". Laura was his sweet faced girl friend and she often rode with him.

One winter day they were on the way to school. It was a bright, frigid morning with 10 inches of snow. The road was snow packed and very icy. It was slicker than a Carney in a sideshow; slicker than owl grease on a doorknob.

They were talking and laughing as they topped a small hill and much to their terror a diesel locomotive was just entering the crossing at the bottom of the hill. The engineer laid on the horn and the moaning, eerie sound rode on the frosty air as he tried to warn them of their impending doom.

Robbie slammed on the brakes. The car slid sideways, bucked and jumped. He tried in vain to stop but they moved relentlessly down the hill. There were patches of stone and ruts in the ice that made the car lurch and career along. He pumped the brakes and down shifted the transmission but the car seemed to speed up. He thought, "We are done for." As the car slid closer and closer to their doom, he thought, "Cars don't fare very well against freight trains."

The "Tank" skated down the hill, sometimes almost sideways. Robbie tried to steer it off into the ditch but the ice was so slick the wheels would not bite and turn. The train loomed larger and larger. Laura felt a sharp, sickening ache in her chest. She was responding physically to imminent danger and very real fear. Her life flashed before her eyes. Robbie yelled, "Hold on, we're going to crash!"

In that agonizing moment they knew that the car and train soon would do the dance of death. Robbie pushed harder on the brake pedal. They held their breaths. Their hearts were in their throats. Laura sank her fingernails so deeply into Robbie's arm that she nearly pinched it off.

Closer and closer they slithered toward their kismet. They were seconds from being maimed or dying. Suddenly and unexpectedly fate intervened on their behalf. The track bed was somewhat higher than the surface of the road as is common in many country crossings. Fortunately someone had spread sand on the incline for traction in crossing the tracks. The front wheels of the "Tank" found the sand, took a bite and stopped. They scarcely breathed. Their hearts were pounding. Fear hung in the air like a bad smell.

The train cars groaned, creaked and swayed as they roared along the old track. The noise was deafening. The "Tank" was so close that the end of each axle on each wheel nicked and nudged the front bumper. It felt like a giant was rocking the car by kicking the bumper every second or so. Another few inches and they would have been doomed.

Finally, after an agonizingly long time, the caboose came by and gave the car a final defiant nudge and went on its way. The signalman riding in the caboose recoiled in surprise to see them sitting that close to the track. Several minutes passed before their heartbeats and breathing returned to a semblance of normal. Even though it was a very cold day, sweat matted Laura's hairline; the drumming sound inside her chest had accelerated until it sounded like a hammering fugue for a kettledrum. Her lips parted but no sound came out, her eyes were two blank orbs. At long last, she relaxed a bit and wheezed, "We can go now."

But Robbie could not move. He was paralyzed, frozen to the seat. The muscles in his face were pulsating, his jaw clenched, his eyes wide, staring at the track. When he spoke his voice was a rippling sheet of ice. He croaked, "I can't move my leg. It won't loosen up so I can move my foot off the brake pedal." They had to sit there for several more minutes before Robbie could relax enough to drive on to school. The first thing he did when he arrived was to wobble into the lavatory and check his Fruit of the Looms.

The Sticker Lady

It was August 12, 1969, a typical hot, humid, muggy Indiana day. It was the kind of day that you perspire just standing in the shade. Wally had just returned home from a two-year hitch in the army. He had no direction in his life and nothing pressing to accomplish that day. So he tagged along with his mother to the neighborhood grocery store just to have something to do and to escape the boredom. He caught up on things he had missed while in the army as they strolled through the aisles of the store. After picking up a few necessities they moved toward the checkout counter. His mother chose register number two and that decision changed his life forever.

They were about fourth in line when he saw "her" for the first time. "Her" was the beautiful young lady working the cash register. She was so pretty that he could hardly take his eyes off of her. As they reached the cash register, Wally battled the urge to stare at her. Within these few minutes, which seemed like a lifetime, he could tell that she had a true concern for everyone. She had something nice to say to each person in her line, especially the kids. He could hear her say things such as "You look pretty," and "Where did you get that outfit?" She had a smile on her face bigger than outside and she was drop dead gorgeous.

Needless to say Wally found many reasons to be in that store after that day. As time went on he saw her continue to give smiles and compliments to everyone and she began to give stickers to the kids. Like Jolly Old St. Nick, she had a clear plastic bag and it was filled with stickers. The customers were so fond of her that it wasn't uncommon to see her line clogged with regular customers while the lines of the other cashiers were empty. If she was not at her register, kids would call out, "Where is the Sticker Lady?" Many times he saw her rush across the store when she heard

77

a child crying, hoping that something in her plastic bag would make things better.

Curiosity got the best of Wally. One day he asked her how she could always be so positive. She said that the smiles from the kids and the customers gave her energy. Then she offered him her formula, which was to say and do three nice things each day for others, and she promised that he too would have more energy. Wally came to realize that if she were to add up all the kind things she said and did each day, that she would generate enough power to light up a small city.

Because of her smile, her attitude and her concern for others, the casual observer would conclude that she didn't have a care in the world except for the well being of the customers. However, one day the Sticker Kids came into the store and they did not see the Sticker Lady. They wanted to know where she was. There was a buzz throughout the store that she was not well. Breast cancer, like a terrorist who strikes so many women without warning, had struck the Sticker Lady. It didn't matter that she was only 32 years old. It didn't matter that she had four children. It didn't matter that so many kids had become dependent on her stickers. It didn't matter that so many people needed her smiles.

But this terrorist didn't realize whom he had chosen to attack. The Sticker Lady was no ordinary target. She would not be a victim.

She traveled the road through the dark forest of surgery and the gloom of chemotherapy and came out on the other side in the sunlit meadow of recovery. Then she came back to the grocery store. She found a huge stack of cards and pictures from friends and her Sticker Kids. She also learned that she had been promoted. Her job description changed and the location of her sticker business changed also. Now she worked in the office that was located in the center front of the store and was raised several feet above the floor.

This location had many advantages. It was as if she had been granted her own watchtower. She now had more space and her sticker business expanded to include small toys, plastic jewelry and fake tattoos.

For the next ten years Wally watched her pass out stickers and hope. She had become a legend. The Sticker Lady was a living testimony that cancer does not have to be a death sentence. She held her own for ten years and didn't let cancer gain any ground. She was the one that so many women and men looked to as an example to help them triumph over the cancer that in some way had attacked their lives too.

However, after one of many routine medical checkups she found that the terrorist had returned. This time he struck through a small spot on her lung. Once again she bravely walked through the darkness of surgery and the gloom of chemotherapy. She took control and returned to her home to recover. Her recovery took longer this time. Four months later, however, the Sticker Kids came into the store and there she was, back on the job in her watchtower. This time she was a little slower but she had an even larger bag of stickers and toys.

She gave more than toys. She and the store had become a lifeline for the community. She was the beacon that gave light and hope to so many that had cancer, to those who would get cancer and to those who knew someone with cancer. And, it is difficult to determine who got more excited; the Sticker Kids who received the stickers or the Sticker Lady who gave them.

The years rolled by and the terrorist has struck a third time. This time it was a tumor in her eye. Surgery was not an option. The doctors called upon the two huge guns of radiation and drug therapy to combat this new wave of terror. The Sticker Lady was told that she could lose her sight as a result of the radiation treatment. She also was told that blindness was lurking around the corner if the tumor continued to grow. Wally remembered thinking, "Could fate be so cruel?" He wondered if the disappointment of not being able to see her Sticker Kids would be more difficult to deal with than the cancer itself.

Many years have rolled by since he first saw "her" on that hot August day at the cash register. Morning follows night, day follows day, year follows year and before you know it, you step across that line into old age. This is the thirtieth year that the Sticker Lady has been coming home to Wally as his wife. And for the past fifteen years she has been waging war against the terrorist and winning. She is at her post daily passing out stickers and she continues to be a beacon of hope for all that she sees. She has truly blessed Wally's life. He enjoys watching her spend hours at the kitchen table organizing, ordering and choosing the perfect stickers for her Kids. He has heard her say many times, "I know just who will like this one." But she is not just giving stickers; she is also giving hope and memories.

Wally sits and watches her and can't help but smile. He is reminded of the song by Tracy Bird that begins with the lines, "It was no accident, me meeting you, someone had a hand in it, long before I ever knew." You see you never know what a simple trip to the grocery store might bring. On that hot and humid August day over 30 years ago, Wally reached into life's grocery sack and found the Sticker Lady who has made his life complete.

The Dirty Rat Let Them Down

What would you do if you were confronted with a rat? I don't mean a friendly looking animal that Disney would draw such as the lovable mouse in the movie Stuart Little. I am talking about a mean, ugly, dirty, menacing rat!

Mike and Cindy were flying by the seat of their pants, taking a leisurely off-season vacation through the Smokey Mountains. Jack Frost had painted the leaves in colors that humans cannot duplicate. They strolled slowly through the days their lungs devouring the crisp autumn air. At dusk, the sky was a painter's pallet as the sun went down in a blaze of color. The smell of wood burning in the fireplace reached out like a golden rope and drew them inside their rustic cabin.

Saturday morning arrived in pink streaks as the mountains could no longer hold back the sun. After breakfast, Mike and Cindy decided to continue their trip. Mike inserted the ignition key to start the car. The engine growled and groaned and refused to run. He tried again and again. Finally, the engine coughed, sputtered and reluctantly started. It wheezed and hacked like a camel caught in a sandstorm. It ran rougher than Main Street in Chuckhole City, Utah, then gasped and died, never to start again.

Acting as if he knew what to do, Mike raised the hood and was confronted by a snarling rat. Alarmed, he stumbled backwards. The rat was sitting on top of the engine. Evidently it had found this warm refuge the night before and wasn't going to give it up easily. From Mike's place of safety, the rat looked larger than a Shetland pony. He yelled at the rat. The rat snarled. He got a stick and poked the rat and kicked the fender. Mr. Rat finally decided to check out. He lunged off the engine, scurried across the fender and scuttled defiantly into the woods.

Mike called every dealer and garage in the immediate area. Both of them. No answer. He called a dealership in the next town about 40 miles distant. A man answered but said that only the sales staff was in and his mechanics didn't work on Saturdays. Finally, Mike persuaded him to see if one of the mechanics would come. "Well, I know this ole boy who lives about an hour or more from you that might help," he said. A short time later the man called back and said the mechanic would come as soon as he could.

The sky darkened and a slow drizzling rain dampened their spirits as they despondently sat and waited. About two and one half-hours later, a mirage of rust and dents emerged out of the rain, lumbered down the street and stopped at the motel. The door of the ancient truck clanged open and Floyd the mechanic, with a smile bigger than all outdoors, creaked out. He carried his 73 years with honor and dignity. Looking at them through cracked and scratched glasses he said, "Hi y'all, are you the ones who called for a mechanic?"

"Yes, we are, thank you for coming," Cindy said.

"What seems to be the problem?"

"I don't know," Mike said and explained what happened. They looked under the hood.

"Right here is your trouble. Mr. Rat has done chewed your sparkplug wires nearly in two and I don't have any with me. Ain't nothin' open in this place. I'll haffta go back to the dealer to get some. Be back shortly."

He was gone an hour or more and when he returned it took him another hour to replace the wires. It was close to three o'clock. He started the engine that now ran like a precision watch. Mike and Cindy were mentally calculating the bill using the factors of Saturday, overtime, the long trip, the trip to get the wires plus the work and then another long trip to get home.

Mike said, "Floyd, you just don't know how much we appreciate you coming out today to help us. We would have been stranded here for at least three more days." Then clutching his checkbook close to his heart and with the chill of expectation filling his stomach, he asked, "How much do I owe you?" Mike had mentally calculated the cost to be at least $400.

Floyd smiled and with rain dripping off the bill of his cap, he said, "Where y'all from?"

Cindy said, "We are from Indiana, near Indianapolis."

"Y'all just visiting down here?"

"Yes, we are and we are really enjoying ourselves. The colors are fabulous and the mountains are a nice change for us."

"Well, you don't owe me a thang. Them was used wires I found. I been in tight spots before and people have helped me. One time we were over there by Knoxville and blew a tire. And I declare our spare was flatter than Kansas, and me a mechanic. Some folks came by, took us into town, got the tire fixed and shared their picnic dinner with us. You can pay me by helping someone else in time of trouble. Now you have a pleasant stay in our state, and come back sometime." And with that he banged the door shut on his rusty steed, and disappeared into the misty rain.

Mike and Cindy were astonished, but right then and there they vowed to pay Floyd by helping someone else.

Chuck Taylor Fouled Out

I was reading the obituary columns the other day in the Indianapolis Star and saw that Chuck Taylor had fouled out of the game of life. Actually I was reading the business section and it wasn't Chuck that fouled out, it was the company that sells Chuck Taylor sneakers. Converse Shoe Company has filed for bankruptcy and moved their production to Indonesia. This is beginning to sound like a broken record. A Company cannot make it in America so it moves offshore.

Reading about Chuck Taylor sent me careening down memory lane to Bloomfield, Indiana. When I was growing up on a farm in Highland Township, our family would go to town to shop. We could go anywhere we wanted as long as it was Worthington and Bloomfield. We purchased most of our clothing in Bloomfield at the Sparks Department Store located off the Northwest corner of the Courthouse Square. The Sparks family, Mom and Pop and their "momettes" and "popettes" owned and operated the store. My mother would still shop there if they were still open. "At least they gave you good service," she says frequently. I agree with her.

As I remember, the ground floor was for women and children. The men and boys' department was in the basement. The second floor was for second floor stuff. When Jimmy Sparks was a teenager, he worked the men's department and sold me a pair of Chuck Taylors. I don't know where any other member of the Sparks family lives now but Jimmy lives near me in Plainfield. I also remember that my mother purchased a pair of black shoes for me to wear while marching with the Mighty Worthington-Jefferson Rambler Band. Since they were new, they wore blisters on my heels that were as large as a balloon in the Macys' Thanksgiving Day Parade.

What are Chuck Taylors? Converse was making tennis shoes in the early part of the last century. Chuck Taylor was quite a high school basketball player in Columbus, Indiana, at the time. After graduating in 1923, he played a bit of professional ball, and then became a hired hand for Converse to sell shoes. He was such a successful salesman that the company put his name on one style of its shoes and ever since they have been known as Chuck Taylors. I have a pair now but they do not resemble the old fashioned, cheap, black shoes of yesteryear.

Everyone wore Converse shoes back then. They became popular again when my daughters were in their teens. Grunge bands and garage bands still wear them. The carcass was black canvas with white shoestrings and eyelets. The shoes had a white toe that resembles the look of a man's wing tip dress shoe. The canvas top was attached to the sole which was a flimsy piece of rubber that was so thin that if you stepped on a chewing gum wrapper you could tell if there was gum in it or not. The tops laced up higher around the ankle and people believed that design would help prevent ankle sprains. It was the innovator Chuck Taylor who made the suggestion to make the higher tops. The shoes had absolutely no arch support. Wearing them gave the same sensation as walking bare footed on concrete. Well, not quite, but almost. The soles had no heel and were flatter than West Texas and Twiggy's chest, if you know what I mean. It was analogous to lacing up a piece of tire tread found along the interstate. They were made of semi-soft rubber that felt like you were walking on a large piece of already chewed bubble gum. However, when a kid laced on a pair of Chucks, that kid felt like an All Star. They were the prehistoric Air Jordans.

When I was in elementary and secondary school no one and I mean no one wore tennis shoes except during physical education classes or when practicing or playing basketball. If you did, it was construed that you were too poor to buy regular shoes. Many of those shoes had black rubber soles and they would make black marks on the gym floor that were as dark as the River Styx. A coach would suffer apoplexy if a player tried to wear those shoes on the floor of his fiefdom.

I remember when basketball teams began to wear all white shoes. They were so "cool." Time out! There are two words, "cool" and "awesome" that are overused. I am asking those people who have influence on the vernacular of America to please generate some new words. Those two words are overused, trite, ordinary, bland, characterless, stale, worn, trivial, dull, boring, cliched, pedestrian, hackneyed, prosaic, facile, insipid and banal. Do you get the impression that I don't like them? You are correct. I have grown weary of hearing them. Now on with the show.

If my memory is correct, the great Indiana legend Larry Bird wore Converse shoes during his career. He was probably paid a handsome sum to do so. I am not sure they were Chuck Taylors, but they were cool.

Chuck's passing saddened me. Reading the story caused me to think about my past and my great athletic career at Worthington-Jefferson High School. It also caused me to remember my illustrious basketball career at Indiana State where I played on the team in the arena. I didn't make the actual college team but I played some pick up games in the arena on weekends and evenings when the team was not using it.

And today as I dribble down the hardwood floor of memory, I remember wearing Chuck Taylors in Physical Education classes and while playing basketball especially in junior high school. But now that I think about it, maybe they were Keds.

Big Bubba Could Wrestle

One of the responsibilities I had each day as an assistant principal in a large high school was noon supervision in the student cafeteria. Some called it guard duty, sentry duty or the watch. I enjoyed it because it provided me the opportunity to talk to students like Bubba. I talked to him just about every day. Bubba was huge but affable which was good. He stood 6' 5" tall and weighed 330 pounds. U.S.S. Bubba left a big wake. He was not exceptionally fit, but he carried his weight quite well. He was solid and strong. He was also a big friendly, funny guy. He was a jokester and an easy laugh. He played a little football in the line but he was too slow to be effective.

Bubba's forte was wrestling - unlimited heavyweight. You didn't think he would wrestle at 138 pounds did you? He always won his matches in the first couple of minutes because he was usually several inches taller and weighed up to eighty pounds more than some of his opponents. His opponents would come out and look up at Bubba, then back at the coach, then look at Bubba, then back at the coach and their body language would be screaming do I have to wrestle this Goliath? Some whimpered when they saw him.

The strategy was always the same. The opponent would go for Bubba's feet in a vain attempt to get him down. Bubba would shuffle backwards just fast enough to evade them. He would then put his massive hands on their shoulders and push them down to the mat and then he would initiate his infamous cannonball belly flop right on the guy. His next move was to assume a very wide base and turn himself in the same direction as his opponent. The opponent would still be on his stomach trying desperately to breathe and wondering what to do with Mt. Bubba on his back! Bubba would hook him in a chicken wing move, turn him over on his back and then continue his flop technique.

The other guy would struggle and struggle against the massive weight. Bubba rode his opponent like a bronco or a steer. He was just agile enough to keep his immense body centered over his opponent with a very strong base position. The other guy would bridge - raise himself using his head and hips to keep his shoulders off the mat - twist and turn, wriggle and struggle but to no avail. When your opponent weighs as much as Bubba, you can only bridge and move so long and then his colossal weight would just paralyze you.

Bubba waltzed his way through his senior year smashing opponents easily. No one could successfully challenge him. His matches were usually concluded in the first round. He strode through the sectional and regional matches like Sherman marching through Georgia. Then came the Saturday semi-state matches in Evansville.

He went off with great confidence and aplomb fully expecting a victory and then on to the state. Monday I was in my usual station in the cafeteria. I saw Bubba. He finished his meal and then came over to where I was standing. He was holding his head very still, he walked with a slight limp and he appeared to have a stiff neck. He was a bit more subdued than usual but he still had a big smile on his face. "Bubba", I said, "How did it go Saturday?" "Not so good," he replied. "Did you win?" Bubba dropped his gaze and said, "I lost in the final match of the day." "I'm sorry, what happened?"

"Well, Mr. V., I walked out on the mat and there for the first time in my life stood a guy as big or bigger than I am. It surprised me. Now I know how those other guys felt when they saw me. We took our best holds and went after it. I would get a grip on him and then he would break my hold and get me in a hold and on and on. We each had some take downs and some reversals. We wrestled for the entire allotted time but he out pointed me for the win. He 'bout broke my neck!"

88

"That's too bad, Bubba. You had a great career in wrestling here, and I am sorry you did not win the state in your last go round."

"Thanks, Mr. V., I had a good run and I am happy with it. Oh, by the way, I know a guy who was so dumb."

"How dumb was he Bubba?" I said rolling my eyes.

"He was so dumb that he thought the county seat was a public toilet."

"That's a hoot, Bubba. Really hilarious! Now get out of here and go to class." He roared with laughter and ambled off down the hallway. I noticed that he was tilted a little to the left. What a great kid.

Call Me A Time Out, Coach

In his former life as he liked to say, James was a high school teacher and a basketball coach. He was the coach for the Tiger junior varsity squad. One cold Indiana evening the Tigers were playing the Eagles from a much larger school and they were getting killed as we say in sports. The Tigers were ragged and flustered and the Eagles were playing with great confidence. By the beginning of the fourth and final quarter, the Eagles were leading by 15 points and the lead was growing.

James had used all of his timeouts and he could only sit and watch the debacle. He knew Wilson, the coach of the other team quite well. They were friends. He walked over near the other bench and asked, "How about calling me a time out, coach, I need to talk to my boys about what they are doing wrong. Maybe we could make the game more interesting. You know that our job as coaches is to help our players improve and grow. How about it?" Wilson looked rather quizzically at him and pondered the request. He looked at the score and reasoned that his Eagles probably had the game in the bag, so he did call a time out.

James talked to the Tigers and they did better. A few minutes later they were only behind eight points. Once again James said, "Wilson, I think my boys are finally figuring out what to do. I need to help them some more. They need to know and understand what they are doing right so we can use this experience in the future. How about calling another time out?"

There were two minutes left in the game. Wilson pondered the request again. He noted that he had an eight point lead. He noted that the crowd was really whooping it up for his squad and thought they would not let them down. He noted that the Eagles were playing with great confidence and teamwork. He recalled being in similar situations himself and a timeout would have helped his team. He reasoned that he could surely call a time out for his friend because there was no way that he could lose this game. If nothing else he could stall and hold the ball and weather the storm. He called time out.

James really encouraged his team and pumped them up. He reminded them where they had been and where they were now. He reminded them that their destiny was in their own hands. He said, "I don't know what the future holds, but I know who holds your future, you do!" He also said, "Look over there at the Eagles. Look how over-confident they look. They think they have already beaten us. They think they have already won the game. Now what are you going to do about that? Let's go out there, play hard and win, and when we do win we will act like gentlemen and congratulate the Eagles for playing a great game."

The Tigers went back out and played like champions. They were possessed. They jumped, they reached, they stretched, they played outstanding defense, they blocked out and rebounded, stole the ball and scored once, twice, three times and before Wilson realized what was happening his lead had vanished to three points. The Tigers scored again and now they trailed by one point. The Eagles had the ball under the Tiger goal. All they had to do was throw the ball in bounds and let the clock run out. Wilson yelled instructions to his team to do just that.

The Tiger crowd was ecstatic. The Eagle crowd was tentative and unsure. The clock showed three seconds to play. James had coached his team for such an occasion as this. Ronnie, his quickest player, knew his assignment. He was to guard the player who was to pass the ball in bounds. He took his position just to the right of his own goal. He jumped at just the right time, intercepted the pass and laid the ball in the goal as the clock expired and won the game by one point. James and the Tigers were elated. Wilson and the Eagles were deflated. The Tiger crowd was cheering wildly. The Eagle crowd was flying low and you would have thought that there was a wake on their side of the gymnasium.

The two well-coached teams lined up in a great display of sportsmanship, shook hands and congratulated each other. James and Wilson shook hands, as friends and competitors should. James said, "Thank you for helping me out. That means a lot to me and the team." Wilson said, "Your team played well and you out coached me. I failed my team, but you deserved to win. Good game." The two old friends walked off the court together.

Get These Nuts Away From Me!

BW and I were driving to New Albany last weekend to visit our unborn grandbaby and to celebrate the natal day [birthday] of TM, our youngest daughter. We left in mid-afternoon for the nearly three hour drive and we had not eaten since breakfast.

I stopped to fuel the car at the Pilot Station on the South side of Indy. For some reason Pilot, Flying J and Swifty always sell gas for up to ten or fifteen cents per gallon cheaper than anyone else does. So I, being of the penurious (cheap) sort, took advantage of the propinquity (closeness) of the Pilot station and stopped for gas.

This isn't Sunday so I do not intend to preach. I'm just going to give you the facts, Ma'am. Tobacco does not entice me. In fact it is the opposite. I am repelled by the smell of tobacco, the taste of snuff and the burning refuse that is called cigars. I can't stand to taste, touch or smell any of those products. They are repugnant and I simply do not understand why anyone would make the conscious decision to inflict their body with the evil weed of nicotine.

I don't consume alcohol in any form. Never have never will. I have never tasted beer. I tasted wine once and it went through my head like a nail from a nail gun. It reminded me of the smell when a Model A car radiator would boil over that had alcohol in it. Champaign? How does anyone drink that vile and malodorous concoction? We were given a bottle when we were in the Hawaiian Islands celebrating one of our anniversaries. We tasted it and poured the rest down the drain. The smell of alcohol products is enough to keep me from drinking. It is especially bad when it is second hand such as on someone's breath or on the ground where it has been deposited from over indulgent drinkers. I got my share of that in the Navy.

As the song goes, I get no kick from cocaine, marijuana, crack or any other controlled substance. I have never had a day so bad or I have never felt so miserable where I thought that ingesting any of those substances would improve my life or state of mind.

Having said all of that, I must confess that peanuts are something else! I don't mean just peanuts. I mean dry roasted peanuts, cocktail peanuts, salted peanuts, smoked peanuts and my all time favorite honey roasted peanuts. They can be quite addicting. Let's cut to the chase, I am addicted. I go to meetings and stand up and say, "Hi, my name is Larry and I am a peanutaholic." If the preacher ever talks about indulging in peanuts I will accuse him of meddling. Our journey continued.

As we drove down the road, we discussed the level of hunger that we were experiencing.

"Are you wanting to eat now or later?"

"Oh, I don't know, how about you?"

"I'm not very hungry, but I could eat something, if you want to."

"Do you want to?"

"I don't know."

"Well, if you want to we better stop soon or it will be too close to dinner time when we arrive."

"I guess I could eat something, but I'm really not too hungry."

"How hungry are you?"

"Oh, I could eat now or wait until we get there."

"What sounds good to you?"

"I don't know, what sounds good to you?"

All married couples get involved in those insipid meaningless conversations on occasions. Some of you perhaps more often. I maintain that if you don't know what sounds good you are not very hungry.

We took a plebiscite, a vote, and decided to delay eating a meal until we arrived in "Nawbany." However, my tummy and taste buds were craving something to eat so while I fueled the car, I entreated BW to purchase some honey-roasted peanuts for me.

She protested quietly knowing how I get when I am eating peanuts. Saints preserve us, not only did she purchase peanuts for me she also purchased a bag of Fiddle Faddle for herself. You know that popcorn with a glaze on it and a few nuts thrown in as an afterthought. That stuff.

We continued down the road munching nuts and fiddle faddling around. Finally, I had eaten all the nuts that was humanly possible, but I couldn't quit. I said I was addicted. So with a demonstration of tremendous mental fortitude and resolve I handed the remaining nuts to BW and said, "Take these peanuts and get them away from me. If I threaten you, don't give them to me. If I threaten to hit you, don't give them to me. If I threaten to beat you, don't give them to me. If I threaten to break your arm and then hurt you, don't give them to me. If I break your glasses and shove them up your nose, don't give them to me. If I try to throw you out of the car, don't give them to me. BUT, if I offer you a $100.00, you might consider giving them to me."

She said immediately, "Show me the money."

Made in USA - Not any More

Is anything made in America any more? The first line of an Oak Ridge Boys song says, "It seems that everything I buy today has a foreign name." They lament about the cars they drive, their video games, Nikon cameras and Sony color TVs. But then they warble about the fact that my baby — significant other — is American made, born and bred in the USA. What a relief!

Each day that I go into the market place I am reminded about how the world is truly becoming a global village. The other day BW was looking at a top that she had purchased. It was a bit too large and she was contemplating sewing it up. The tag said Made in Guatemala. It seems like most of the clothing sold in America is made in Taiwan, Mexico, Korea, Indonesia, or The Philippines. I haven't seen that ad for the Garment Makers Union on TV for a long time. There probably aren't any in America any more. I believe the last shoe manufacturing plant ceased operations some time ago. Even the tennis shoes that we wear are made in some sweatshop in Burma.

I went to "Wally World", Wal-Mart, to look at an exercise weight machine. You know Wally World who used to advertise that we sell only American made products. Look again Pilgrim, the weight machine was made in China.

A couple of years ago BW and I were celebrating our 35th wedding anniversary in the Hawaiian Islands. Believe it or not it gets quite hot there. My almost de-thatched dome looked like an overdone tortilla. I paid $5.00 for a straw hat that was designed in Australia, manufactured in China and sold in Hilo, Hawaii.

About a year ago our water heater began to irrigate the utility room. We shopped around for a new one and discovered that many of the name brands that are so American sounding are now manufactured in Mexico. GE, a mainstay in Indiana manufacturing for many years, closed their operations in Bloomington in favor of a Mexican plant. Phillips, a French Company, now owns venerable RCA that began in Bloomington. I understand that they no longer manufacture anything in Indiana. When the Hoosier Dome became the RCA Dome, those workers who were laid off from RCA were understandably incensed. So was I.

In September 2000, BW and I were motoring down a four-lane highway. I sat fat, dumb and happy in the passenger seat while she drove. Suddenly a truck careened across three lanes and the median and TKO'd her two-year old Ford Escort Zx2. The other driver was at fault. We were not hurt, thanks to air bags and seat belts, but the car was totaled. As a result of this carnage, get it carnage, we had to replace our car. We took the laughable settlement into the market place. The blue book value of the car was lower than the GNP of an iceberg. It was valued about the same as a bowl of noodles in a Thailand fast food shop.

Grumbling all the way, we added 3K to the settlement and bought a Chevrolet Lumina that was one year newer than the Escort. I felt good about buying an American car. You cannot get any more American than Chevrolet. Later I glanced at a plate on the door and it said ASSEMBLED IN CANADA. Aargh!

Just try to buy a camera, a computer an electronic game or anything in that line of products that is made in America. There are some, but expect to see Japan or Taiwan on the label. The School Corporation where I was formerly employed purchased a large quantity of IBM computers. I looked down inside the casing of one of them and in bold letters was a sign, Assembled in Ireland and they didn't mean Ireland, Indiana. America even imports 50% of its petroleum from OPEC who is going to cut production this week.

When we were in Europe last year, our tour guide, who was British, said that she had recently visited America.

While on the West Coast she began to look for gifts, mementos and souvenirs that were made in America. She laughed and stated that in every gift shop, most of the products were made in Europe or Asia. I asked her if she had thought about our burgers and fries. She thought that was a hoot.

As I have contemplated this dilemma, several conclusions have piled up in my brain. America does not hold a corner on quality and production. Other lands have hard working people who do quality work for less money. American companies are using that cheap labor to enhance profits at the expense of the American worker. The world community is becoming more and more interdependent for goods and services to satisfy an ever-demanding marketplace.

I have a suggestion for a new label to be sown into clothing or attached to durable goods that are sold in America. It would read **USA but MSE**, which means Used and Stored in America, but Made Somewhere Else.

Claude Pepper, We Are Here

[If you do not know who Claude Pepper was, stop reading now because the rest of the article will not amuse you. I mean it, stop reading now. If you continue reading, the staff and management of this column will not assume any liability for the consequences you may suffer and we will disavow any right to litigation on your behalf.]

I received my first AARP (American Association of Retired Persons) card when I reached the age of 50. It didn't matter that I had not and did not plan to retire then. I am not proud, though, I gladly accepted the benefits the magic card provided. Membership provides discounts on motel rooms and some airline tickets, discounts in some restaurants and theaters, lower car insurance, prescription drug delivery to your door at a lower price and information on how to purchase a scooter or to determine if you qualify to have it paid for by Medicare. Now I just ask clerks and other service personnel to use my face as verification that I am a senior citizen. No one has challenged me in many years.

In recent years BW and I have concluded that old people like to travel in the "off season". We made that conclusion last October when we were in Branson, Missouri. Why do you think we were there? AARPers can travel then because they are retired and have earned the right to take a trip anywhere they please any time they please. There should be some benefit to living a long time, don't you agree?

AARPers were everywhere. There is more gray hair in Branson in October than there is snow on the Matterhorn in January. Branson streets and venues resemble a white out in a blizzard from September through December. Those life time membership AARP cards were getting heat rash or razor burn from being whipped through the scanners at the malls and restaurants and being presented for discounts at motels and RV parks. Some disappeared in a cloud of smoke because of spontaneous combustion. Most stores have a barrel of water near the cash register to serve as a coolant. It reminded me of Gar Wells' blacksmith shop in Worthington years ago. Steam would fly and the water would hiss when he put horseshoes and plowshares in his water barrel to cool them.

AARPers are the reason that the has-beens of the entertainment world are fixtures in Branson. AARPers are the only ones who know or remember Bobby Vinton, Andy Williams, Jim Stafford, The Osmond Brothers, Tony Orlando and Sunset (get it?), The Lawrence Welk Show, Mickey Gilley and Mel Tillis. They all have their AARP cards too and most of them have restrictions on their driver's license that prohibits them from driving after dark. That is why their shows end so early.

There were so many fifth wheel campers, RVs, tent campers and other styles of camper vehicles in town that it looked like a RV dealership on the move. On the road to Branson we passed so many that it looked like the Union Pacific Railroad Line.

We never saw so many double knit suits, double knit pants, horn rim glasses, hard side suitcases and overnight cases since the 1970's or was it in Florida the winter before?

I'll bet my next paycheck against yours that there were more pacemakers than pace arrows in town. There was enough nitroglycerine and cholesterol lowering medicine in pockets and purses to stock a regional distribution center for CVS Drug Stores. Sales of kaopectate and milk of magnesia are the highest per capita there than anywhere except Florida and Sun City, Arizona. Senior citizen drug pushers blatantly sell over-the-counter drugs out of the trunks of their cars right there on the streets. Every restaurant and buffet line has drums of industrial strength Pepto-Bismol at the cash register.

Traffic is terribly congested in Branson. It is slower than Ameritech's schedule to install a new phone line in Indianapolis. It takes longer to drive a block in Branson than it took for the 2000 presidential election. There is a local law that states: "No driver shall exceed five miles per hour; drivers must hold one foot on the brake pedal with the brake lights on just in case; drivers must keep at least one turn signal blinking just in case they might want to turn sometime in the next three hours. If a driver is unsure of which way he or she is going to turn, then said driver must keep the hazard lights flashing just in case. Stopping in the middle of the road to read maps and determine the location of the next buffet is permissible as long as you intend to move on in the next two hours."

We noticed that there is no late nightlife in Branson. Everything closes after Andy Williams' last show. Silver Dollar City closes at 5:00 to insure that all ticket holders can get back to town in time to take their pre-dinner heartburn medicine and Lipitor tablets. The streetlights go off at 9:00 p.m. Senior citizens on the streets after that are given a free ride in the nice policeman's car or the local 911-rescue unit to the nearest medical facility because it is assumed that they must be confused and lost.

BW and I will go to Branson again this fall but I must get my leisure suits washed and ironed before we go. I also have to get my prescription of Lipitor renewed. It seems that one of our turn signal bulbs is burned out too. Must get that replaced and purchase a drum of Grecian Formula, and we are off.

(Claude Pepper was a congressional leader from Florida who was a champion for senior citizens and their rights. He died a few years ago. I knew you wouldn't stop reading.)

Hi Gwampuh

Tom drove his old pickup truck down the road through the swirling snow. He was on his way to Bloomington, Indiana. The old truck had been his faithful friend for many years. It was the only vehicle he allowed himself since that fateful day four years ago. The scene was burned into his mind as if it were yesterday. It seemed like a slow motion movie. The driver of a huge coal truck, who was doped up on drugs, lost control of the behemoth, crossed the centerline and smashed into his car. The car was a total wreck. So was his life. Although the truck driver stumbled away unharmed, Ann's life was snuffed out like a candle when the door is opened and the winter wind slips inside.

Reverie overtook him for a moment as Tom thought about the 33 happy years they had sailed in a boat of love across the ocean of life. The steering wheel jerked in his hands and brought him back to the present. Both he and the truck fought the wind. The old truck fishtailed and slid valiantly struggling against the grip of Old Man Winter. Tom wrenched the wheel, the tires caught and the truck righted itself and resumed its way down the snow carpeted road. The windshield wipers fought gamely against the snow and at that moment Tom was unsure which was going to win the battle of supremacy. The heater pumped warm air into the cab in sharp contrast to the razor sharp wind outside.

Ann's death had been a crushing blow that almost took his life also. Not long after that another devastating blow was delivered to his life. Madison —Maddie— his only daughter and youngest child drove a dagger into his heart. One day she called Tom and told him that she had decided to drop out of Indiana University and marry Jimmy. Jimmy was an all right boy but he had very little going for him. Tom had high hopes for Maddie, hopes that included a better life than he had. He and Ann had dreamed that their children would have happy, prosperous lives. They had scrimped and saved to send all of the children to college with the hope of good careers. Joey and Kevin had done so. But Maddie, the youngest had defied him and dropped out to marry an ex-Navy man, a part-time student, who had a dead-end job, low income and no future. Nothing could dissuade her.

Tom had talked until he was blue in the face but Maddie did not listen. He begged her to reconsider, but she was in love with the boy. She was travelling Love Street on the way to bliss and nothing could stop her. One thing led to another and anger grew in Tom's heart. He said hurtful things. He threatened to remove her from his life. He yelled, "After all I have done for you and you are just going to throw it all away! For what? Nothing but a guy with a big smile. I taught you better than that. You deserve better than that. I'm just glad that your mother is not here to see this. It would break her heart." Then Tom drew the line in the sand. His pride took over. He snarled, "It's either him or me. Take your pick." In matters of the heart, reason must ride in the back of the bus. Your own children will fight when they are pushed into a corner. Maddie's heart caused her to pick Jimmy.

It does not matter how large or how small your house is, there is always room for pride to move in and stay. Pride is a huge, smelly, rude, arrogant beast that lives in many hearts and houses. It keeps people apart and causes hate to proliferate among family and friends. If it were a plant it would be Kudzu or Johnson Grass. It is the dagger that kills friendships. It is the battleship that blasts families to pieces. The tragedy is that many people cannot even see the beast, but it is there. Others see it but they will not admit seeing it. Pride and Tom were roommates for a long time.

Two years had passed since that fateful day. Tom had not seen Maddie in that time even though only 30 miles separated them. She had married the guy and even had a baby that he had never seen. One day Joey told him that Jim had graduated from technical school and had a good job with a bright future. He had let the news blow away like so much chaff in the wind. Maddie wrote him occasionally and sent him birthday cards and Christmas cards. Some of them he read but most of them remained unopened on his dresser. He had ignored her until now.

On this day, Tom had had an epiphany. The hole in his heart had grown so large that he could not stand it any more. He had to do something. It was something about the Christmas season that caused his heart to melt. He thought about his life with Ann, Maddie, Joey and Kevin. How warm and glorious those years had been. Christmas had been special times for the family. He remembered holding Maddie in her flannel jammies while they looked at the tree with the twinkling lights and pondered what might be in the gaily wrapped presents. He remembered how difficult it was for her to wait for the magic morning to open them. He remembered the overwhelming joy of Christmas mornings. His whole body was tense with regret. His heart ached.

He drove on through the blowing snow. He realized that he had to get his life in order or at least try. The TV weatherman had gravely warned the viewers that this storm could turn into a blizzard by the time it was finished. Three inches of the downy substance already covered the countryside and it did not show signs of stopping. Tom squinted and leaned closer to the windshield but he still had difficulty seeing as the snow swirled and danced sideways across the road in the whirling wind.

Finally, Tom stood outside the apartment where they lived. The wind yanked on his coat and tugged at his cap as the snow swirled about him. Fearful of what lay ahead, he pushed the doorbell not knowing what to expect. At that moment he felt as powerless and insignificant as the referee feels in a professional wrestling match. The door opened and Maddie peered out into the wintry blast.

The world stopped. His heart ached but he could not look at her. His eyes were downcast, his shoulders stooped. He heard himself say in a still small voice, "Maddie, I'm sorry. I don't know what came over me. I lost my way for a while, but sometime if you can see your way clear to let me, I want to be part of your life again. I know that I don't deserve it and I have no right to ask. I am so terribly sorry for what I did and what I said. Please forgive me." The words fought through the wind to get to her ears.

Much to his surprise, Maddie shrieked, "Oh, daddy, daddy, yes, yes, I have prayed for his moment." She leaped barefooted out into the snow and hugged him. She didn't even feel the cold snow on her feet. Finally, she said, "Come in, come in." They stepped inside the little apartment so filled with warmth and love. Jimmy, her husband said, "Welcome, Tom and Merry Christmas." The world began to turn again.

Tom glanced around the modest apartment through eyes filled with tears of uncertainty and saw the small, gaily-trimmed tree and the presents spread around. Jim strode across the room and returned with a bundle of wiggles wrapped in yellow flannel jammies, wearing Johnson & Johnson perfume. He held the bundle out to Tom and said, "Julie, this is your Grandpa. Say hi to Grandpa." Tom could hardly breath as he clutched Julie to his heart. He felt her little head snuggle against his neck and under his chin. Her blonde hair moved as he exhaled. He was swept back to the times when he held his precious Maddie. As Jimmy hugged Maddie she clasped her hands together on her heart and huge tears of supreme joy cascaded down her cheeks.

Julie's little arms hugged Tom's neck and then she leaned back and with her chin nearly touching his and with one tiny hand on each side of his face and her eyes shining like stars in the summer night, she said the magic words, "Hi, Gwampuh."

The Sounds of Grandma's House

Grandmothers are special. They let you play in the cabinets among their pots and pans. They let you help sew on the new sewing machine and if you should happen to throw the adjustments out of kilter they don't seem to care. You can play the piano as long as you like. If you should happen to break something they don't seem to mind as much as parents do.

I remember my Grandma Van who was a widow for many years. She lived in a small white house near Calvertville, Indiana, and I remember the sounds of her house. When I was a child growing up in the 1940s and 50s, life was quite different. Life was slower paced. Activities were different. People were more attached to a place and they didn't venture far from home. Don't be deluded, life was not easy. It never has been. Mayberry does not exist. People worked hard and diseases plagued them as they plague us — some of the ones they contended with, no longer bother us. Interpersonal relationships were bothersome then as now. One aspect of life was much different then and that is sounds in the house.

The sounds in houses were different. Houses were much quieter. If one were to compare houses then to houses now, Grandma's house was a veritable mausoleum. Grandma did not have a washer and a dryer that hummed and growled and thumped through the laundry almost every day, unless you consider the sheets snapping on the solar-powered clothesline on a windy day. She did not have central heating with the rumbling furnace and the humming blower or central air conditioning with the grumbling compressor and the fan blowing cool air. She didn't have a microwave oven with its fan and electronic signal that dings when the popcorn is finished. She didn't have a television set that ran all day and night as background noise. She had no record player, CD player, radio, boom box or other sound producing instruments. Neither did she have a refrigerator or freezer or an electric water pump. She didn't have a computer with clacking printer or annoying electronic games that reverberate throughout houses of today. Her computer and printer were a pencil and a piece of paper. She didn't even have an inside toilet. There was a dearth of sounds in her house.

She had two sounds in her house though that I don't hear any more: a yellow singing canary and a ticking clock. Many people had those two items in their homes of yesteryear. If they were present in houses of today they could not be heard above the din.

Each day the canary would doff its top hat and cane, take its position center perch and sing and dance for her. I made that up about the hat and cane. She would talk to Tweetie, feed her and clean her cage. And for those amenities, Tweetie entertained her and lessened the quietude of the day. I can still hear it chirping and tweeting. I don't remember the last time I saw a bird in someone's house.

Grandma also had a large clock that sat on the mantle. It sat there and tick tocked through the day and night counting the minutes of life. It would also sound the alarm when it was time to arise for the day. As a child I sat in grandma's living room many Sunday afternoons and listened as the adults conversed. Interspersed with the words was the ticking of the clock. When a lull occurred, the clock kept on ticking. The same air that carried the words carried the ticking of the clock, the chimes on the quarter hour and the bonging on the hour. One other sound that I remember was the creaking sounds of Grandma's chair as she rocked.

How I wish that I could go back and sit in Grandma's lap and hear the singing canary and the ticking of the mantle clock. More than that, I wish I could hear her pleasant laughter and listen to her tell about the old days before the turn of the century — the 20th century.

I Waited for the Magic to Return

Main Street USA. It is an idyllic and nostalgic place. A journey down Main Street USA can take you back to a time you may not want to leave. I took such an excursion beginning at Washington and Main beside the former Rexall Drug Store in my home town of Worthington, Indiana. I will never forgive or forget that it was CVS that bought and subsequently closed the Rexall Pharmacy which I am sure was a good business move but a bad public relations move. I passed where Madge Gantz had a beauty shop and then the old Times office. The Christian Church and the Methodist Church were next. The offices of the doctors Moses and Dr. Dyer were next and on down the way at Dayton Street I stopped and reflected about the old two-story brick school building that once stood there. The music room remains and I have fond memories of that place. Ask me about that sometime. The old school was the bastion of education for students in the township. Built in 1875 for the princely sum of $16,000, it remained in service for the next 80 years. And who can forget "My Store" that was across the street from the school. Ah yes, Mrs. Davis, I remember you well. About six blocks farther West on Main, the gymnasium, circa 1941, remains because it was incorporated into the new school in 1955-56.

My destination, however, was at the West End of Main Street — the field adjacent to the current school building. When I was a child my brother and I would accompany our dad to local baseball games on Sunday afternoons. Worthington had a team and it played on that field. I remember Bill Dixon, Bobby Rogers, Wallace Short, Lloyd Rollison and Truman Scharr playing. One time I retrieved a foul ball. The catcher said, "Throw it to me, "Cotton Top." I wound up and gave it my best throw but the ball didn't go where I wanted it to go. How embarrassing!

I stood out on the field that is now a school athletic field and remembered the magic that transcended baseball. I played on the high school baseball team on this very field. The dust of memory swirled through my mind as I stood and waited for the wonderment to return. That field was a place of enchantment in my youth - a field of dreams for other reasons.

Every summer that field was transformed into a magnet that attracted people from all over the county. The magnet was the Greene County Fair. The excitement began to mount months before as people prepared the plethora of exhibits including vegetables, baking, canning, sewing and animals. The carnival moved in and heralded the excitement of the good times ahead. Early in the week Main Street became the Yellow Brick Road for a parade that rivaled the Rose Parade. BW and I have a film of the parade in the early sixties.

Anticipation was rampant. The animal tents were crowded with animals and their owners. It was exciting to stay overnight at the fair and bunk in with Howard, Harold, Gene, Bill and Bob. We all had animals and other exhibits at the fair. I remember my Guernsey calf was awarded a white ribbon but the next week at the 4-H Fair she took home a blue. What times we had roaming the grounds and basking in the garish glow of the midway lights. One night a thunderstorm dumped enough water on the grounds to drown a duck. Water collected in the corner of the cattle tent roof and we feared the weight might pull the tent down. We pushed up on the reservoir of water with our hands and with a pole to no avail. Harold Harper, who was one of the more rambunctious guys, slit the canvas with his genuine Barlow knife and let the water pour out.

Other venues at the fair included a farm machinery field, horse pulling contests and later tractor pulls, animal judging and showmanship contests. I remember the smells of cotton candy, deep fat fried fish, hot dogs, sawdust and plain old dust. And, who can forget the smell of used hay around the animal tents. I also remember the steady drone of the huge generator that supplied the power for the midway.

There was a grandstand for entertainment. I remember one particular year the Hinds girls - Sally, Peggy, and Nadine - sang Via Con Dios. A teenage boy from Coal City played the accordion and sang the Elvis hit "Teddy Bear" and the German Band played, starring yours truly. Another time a gospel quartet from Bloomington performed with one of the WTTV radio personalities as the bass singer. A Dixieland Band from Ft. Thomas, Kentucky, performed one year. Their first number was Muskrat Ramble. What memories of days gone by.

There are few scenarios more forlorn than a fairground and carnival in the bright sunlight. However, at night when it is filled with people under a canopy of stars it becomes an enchanting place. Hear the organ music of the carousel and the shouts and laughter of children. See clusters of socializing friends and bask in the glow of the starry-eyed girl carrying the huge stuffed Teddy Bear that her "feller" won at the strong man booth. Just try to ignore the barker striving to entice you into the sideshow. I can still hear the cacophony of sounds created by the tilt-a-whirl, the Ferris wheel, the chair swings and the carousel.

As those thoughts flooded through the rivers of my memory, I stood and waited for the magic to return, but it never did. The fair only exists in memory's trunk that is stored in the attic of my mind. The trip back up Main was twice as long.

Let's Go Pick Berries

Some of my fondest memories of growing up revolve around the kitchen. Stepping into the kitchen was like stepping into a bakery, a smokehouse and a vegetable garden all at the same time. The room was redolent with the aromas, smells and emanations that come from the process of cooking. Few places in this world are as inviting and warming as a kitchen with loved ones gathered round. The wonderful fragrance of the food pulls me in. The friendship and camaraderie draw me closer. The laughter is like a wind chime on a soft summer evening. Sharing and caring bind hearts together like no Elmer's glue ever could.

We lived in an old farmhouse with a huge kitchen. At one time there was a pantry across the south end of the room. Mom and Dad placed the cream separator in there until we added a room on the North side of the house. As a child one of my jobs was to turn the crank of that device as it separated the cream from the milk. How that happened escapes my feeble attempts to understand, but cream came out of one spout and skim milk came out of another. Lest you think I am as dumb as a box of rocks, I know about centrifugal and centripetal forces, but it remains a mystery to me.

I remember a wood burning stove mom used for cooking and heating that part of the house. Later we burned some coal in it also. When we finally got electricity and an electric stove, mom kept the old stove for heat and she just liked to cook some things on it better than the electric stove.

The joy of stepping into that kitchen when mom was cooking is etched into the windowpane of my mind. The smell of fresh baked bread hung in the air like expensive Parisian perfume. Pavlov's dogs never salivated as I did when mom was baking a ham or a turkey along with vegetables and a boiled blackberry cobbler. When dinner or supper was ready the five of us would crowd around the

112

table like hogs at the trough. We laughed and ate until we would almost burst. I don't ever remember going hungry except between meals. My mom used to laugh and say that my brother and I had at least one hollow leg each that she had a hard time keeping full of food. One thing mom never had to contend with very much was the care and keeping of leftovers. We just didn't have any.

Mom made the best berry pies and cobblers. Roslyn Bakeries and Sara Lee could not hold a candle to her baking. There is a term for you — hold a candle. Does anyone know what that means? Write me if you do. I really enjoy eating berries. I did then and I still do today. There are few food items more succulent and scrumptious than strawberries, blackberries and raspberries.

We had all three on our farm. We also had cherry, peach, pear and persimmon trees but that is another genre of mouth watering food items. Let the record show that I hated picking all three berries but the record should also show that I enjoyed eating them and the jellies, cakes, pies, cobblers and jams made with them.

Farming was and still is to a certain extent hard work. It was much harder back then because everything was low tech and required much manual labor. I dreaded the day when dad would say, "Let's go pick berries." It was never a request. It was not a suggestion. It was not open for debate. There was no forum for a discussion about whether we wanted to go or not. It was a statement of fact — Let's go pick berries. So, we went.

Berries ripen in the summertime. Strawberries come first in late May or early June. Blackberries and raspberries come later in June or July. Indiana summer days are hot and muggy. The old timers would say it is close. Heat and humidity were as inescapable as acne on a teenager's face. They hang in the air like cigar smoke in a Teamsters Meeting.

So, it was always a hot day when dad said lets go pick blackberries or raspberries. We would put on our armor like knights going to a joust. The shields and protective clothing we wore were meant for protection and not necessarily for comfort. It certainly was not a fashion show. We wore long sleeved shirts to protect our arms and wrists from scratches from the briars. We pulled on two pairs of overalls to protect our legs and torsos from the rapier-like gouges of the thorns. Brown brogan shoes protected our feet. We would tie the cuffs of the overalls tight around the ankles to keep the legs down and to keep varmints from infesting our ankles. Some people would tie kerosene soaked rags around their ankles to keep the chiggers away. We then tied a red bandana around our necks and put on a cap to protect our heads. A belt or baling twine was tied around our waist from which hung the small pail to hold the berries. With that many clothes on in mid July, I would be sweating like President Clinton trying to explain what "is," meant.

Every time we went to pick berries there was always at least one encounter with a snake either a black snake or a blue racer. Sometimes a garter snake would venture by to see what we were doing. The cows, who had enough sense to stay in the shade, would look at us with quizzical expressions as we passed. I'm sure they had a conversation after we were out of earshot. "Did you see those crazy humans? Why do they have on all those extra clothes?" "I don't know. Didn't their mothers teach them to stay out of the sun on such hot days?" "They don't have the sense that God gave geese and you know how silly they are. They look goofier than that unblinking Steve Forbes making a political speech. Hah, hah, hah." I'll bet they laughed harder at us than Red Skelton did at his own jokes.

It did not matter how much armor I had on, I got stuck more times than the IRS at tax time. I looked like I had lost a fight with Edward Scissorhands. Dad seemed impervious

114

to scratches and bites. He would wade into the patch and work assiduously. Brother and I worked sort of assiduously. Berries, especially raspberries, are so small that it takes two gazillion of them to fill a quart berry pail. It took me 10 days to get one pail full. It seemed to me that Dad would empty his half-gallon pail into the ten-gallon reserve bucket every two minutes.

Sweat would pour out of my body like insults pour out of the crowd at a high school basketball game as the people vilify the referee. The sweetest words ever heard in the universe was when Dad would finally say, "Well, boys what do you say? Have you had enough berry picking for the day?" "Yes," we would groan like frogs in the summer night. "Well, let's go to the house." He did not have to say it twice.

Mom would take those berries and make a pie that was ambrosia. Our family could consume one twelve-inch pie per meal. We prepared the berries and froze them so like the ant we could eat them throughout the winter until the next time Dad would say, "Let's go pick berries." I wish we could go pick again. I wouldn't complain. I promise.

Summer Symphony of Sound

I grew up out in the country in Highland Township during the transition period between horse power and tractor power. It was a time when farmers in our area were changing over from muscle power to internal combustion power; from hay burners to gasoline burners; from protein power to internal combustion power. Most farmers had purchased at least one small tractor but they still used horses to assist in the many tasks of farming. As time moved on, the horses were phased out except for the die-hards who kept them to plow the garden or to help in putting up hay. I have fond memories of that time.

BW and I recently attended the Rushville Steam Engine and Antique Tractor Show. I truly walked down nostalgia road and was swept away on the winds of reverie as I walked through the fields where the tractors were on display. I found every tractor that was used by every farmer in our community when I was a child. They were so small compared to the behemoths used on the huge farms of today. BW asked, "How do you remember what kind of tractor everyone had when you were a boy?" I do because it was important to me at the time. And just as people recognized the horses that others rode or farmed with in previous generations, tractors identified who you were. Dad, Bert Davis, Kerry Stantz, Uncle Frank and the Osborns drove Farmalls. The Binghams and Pickards drove John Deere tractors and equipment. Irvin Brown and Rex Wilson drove Allis Chalmers, the Thompsons drove Massey Harris and John and Don Calvert had Fords. And now, back to the story.

It was a more peaceful time before electricity and television. Families were closer. People worked hard every day to extract a living from the earth. In the evening after supper families would gather on the front porch to escape the heat. There they talked about the day and about life.

116

Neighbors would often visit and the conversations would revolve around the heat, rain, how the crops looked this year, politics and people.

Many an evening of my youth was spent sitting on the front porch or out in the yard listening to adults talk and listening to the symphony of sounds that permeated a soft summer evening. The moon would bathe the landscape in a soft buttermilk glow that showed the softer side of the universe in well-defined contrast to the sharpness that the sunshine revealed during the day. My brother and sister and I would often chase lightning bugs trying to figure out what made them light.

Sitting on the porch or out in the yard I could hear the horses chuckling and nickering to each other under their breath after they had eaten and drunk their fill and rested after a long hard day of work. One evening ritual was to close the chicken house door to keep foxes and other predators out. The chickens roosted and quietly clucked and sang lullabies. Out in the woods the whippoorwills called to their mates.

About a mile away, beyond the White River that lay across the landscape like a glistening ribbon in the moon glow, I could hear the muffled sound of a steam locomotive clicking and clacking over the steel rails on the Big Four Line. The engine would chuffa chuffa chuffa, its plaintive whistle warned of its approach as it shoved its way through the darkness on the way to Indianapolis.

Down in the pond and along the creek the frog band would tune up their instruments and begin to play. They would thump, harump and garump through their musical score in perfect synchronization. The inevitable squadron of mosquitoes whined and droned in my ear as they sought to draw my blood into their insatiable stomachs. Crickets chirped their end of the day messages to all who cared to listen. The seven-year locusts or cicadas contributed their singsong sounds to the symphony.

Down in the river bottom, on the Osborn farm, Loyal and Kenneth worked late trying to get the corn planted before the rain. Their tractor lights shone weakly as they battled against the darkness that shrouded them. The steady drone of the engines rode to our ears on the soft summer breeze.

Pigs grunted as they lay in their mud wallow or in their houses. Some would still be nuzzling through a late supper or snack so the thumping and banging of the metal lids on the hog feeder added the sound of percussion to the symphony. In the early evening up on the hill behind the house a squirrel barked and chattered over his delightful repast of mulberries before going to bed. Quails called to other members in the troop as they bedded down for the evening. Hoot owls hooted their messages in the quiet evening. Out behind the barn in the old dead tree by the creek, a woodpecker sounded like he was playing a snare drum as he chiseled grubs and insects out of the rotting trunk. Tree frogs croaked in the peach tree. A calf bawled for his mother in the overnight pasture. Momma cow mooed reassuringly and they found each other.

Down across the river bottom and over the distant hills, heat lightning flashed softly as if someone were taking flash pictures too far away for us to see. The low, rumble of thunder flowed through the hills and "hollars" announcing a coming rain. A sudden burst of wind carried on its breath the sweet scent of the land being washed by the approaching rain. The rain began with a few huge drops splattering on the roofs and road. At first it was the dripping sound of a faucet in the bathtub as large drops fell around us. They were the vanguard that announced the imminent arrival of the storm. Then it became a light shower, gently falling through the leaves and dampening the grass.

Another burst of wind made the curtains billow out in the house and a door slammed making us jump. We all ran to gather some remaining wash off the line as it flapped and flailed against the fearful wind. Lightening cracked and flashed much closer now and the thunder boomed defiantly through the river bottom. The rain intensified making a frying, sizzling sound as it fell through the leaves of the maples, tulip poplars and walnut trees in the yard and around the barn. A few hailstones clattered and banged on the aluminum barn roof. We hurried inside to keep from getting wet as the much-needed rain made the countryside cool to the touch which helped us sleep through the night.

Such was the evening symphony of soothing, summer sounds in the country of my youth.

How to Recognize a Geezer!

In a previous column I announced that I am now living with a grandmother. Is it just me or are grandmothers younger and much more beautiful and vibrant than they were when I was a kid? I wonder why? That causes a dilemma in conversations.

The thought has occurred to me that sometimes you might not know if you are talking to a Geezer because they can disguise themselves. It is important to know since geezers and normal people don't use the same vocabulary and one must learn to compensate for the dearth of knowledge that non-geezers have. How do you know you are talking with a Geezer?

Geezers say, "I won't ride with Esther any more because she can't see or hear. Everybody in town cringes when they see Arthur coming. He is going to kill someone some day and get himself killed in the process."

Conversations are like instant replay on television. Do not be alarmed if you didn't hear it the first time, invariably someone will say, "What" or "Huh", and the statement will be replayed; sometimes more than once. But no one needs a hearing aid, right?

Geezers amuse themselves differently. Most senior centers have connect-the-dot day where people use magic markers to connect the liver spots on the back of their hands. One old guy I know claims that he can outline Uncle Sam on his hand. Okay, it is me.

Last night you watched Survivor or Son of The Beach or Baywatch or Sex in the City. You ask, "Did you see the show last night?" The person replies, "Yes I did. That Goober is so funny. Or, isn't Nellie a hateful little girl?" An alarm sounds in your head that the person you are talking to is a Geezer. The Geezer stated that he also watched Mary Tyler Moore, Lawrence Welk, Leave it to Beaver, I Love Lucy and the Waltons. If you didn't know that Goober is in the Andy Griffith Show and Nellie is in Little House On The Prairie, you are not a Geezer.

Then you hear the Geezer mantra that none of those other shows are fit to watch. There is too much sex, violence, vulgarity and profanity in those filthy shows. Many geezers feel that the "Waltons" have almost crossed the line now with Jimmy Bob playing his guitar in a roadhouse and the two sisters making the recipe. They are moonshiners. Everyone just looks the other way because they are nice little old ladies. Many geezers don't realize that the Waltons are in syndication now and that John Boy is 77 years old and living on social security in Brooklyn in a room that you pay by the week.

Geezers are out of the fashion loop. Calvin Klein, Boss, Old Navy and Abercrombie and Fitch are just people they went to school with or who were in the service with them. If the person you are speaking to is wearing a leisure suit or double knit bell bottomed pants and platform shoes, you are walking the streets of "Geezerville."

Geezers take a lot of medicine. They all have those specially manufactured containers with days of the week embossed on the flip top lids. If the lid is up and the box is empty they know they have taken their medicine. And, if they go anywhere, they carry their medicine in those hard-side blue or green Samsonite overnight cases with a mirror in the lid. Geezers go into great detail about the many times they have been "under the knife". Katie bar the door, is that an indication that the writer is a Geezer, if a Geezer has hyperactoliphomea!

Geezers transfuse every conversation with out of left field statements such as, "Did you hear that Charlie dropped dead out in the barn?" Or, "Did you know that Phil and Phyllis are neither one well?" And, "The doctor opened Ned up and just sewed him back together." Plus, "Did you hear that Lois is going in for hemorrhoid surgery tomorrow in Bloomington?"

You know you are in Geezerville when there is something wrong with every restaurant in the area. They say such things as we went to Bob's "Gravy over Everything" Café once and the food was so cold we couldn't eat it and the waitress added the tip onto the bill for our group of 18 and some people didn't like it. Or, the service is too slow, the food isn't cooked properly, they serve booze, they are closed on Monday or Tuesday, portions are too large or too small, overpriced, too smoky, the silverware isn't clean and their instant tea tastes like alfalfa water.

Now you should be able to identify a Geezer? All together now, *I'm a Geezer, she's a geezer, he's a geezer, wouldn't you like to be a Geezer too?* This has been a public service announcement.

That Put The Rag on the Bush
"Warsh" Day in the Good old days

"Warsh" day was usually Monday in the good old days on the farm North of Calvertville. Not for everyone, but it seemed like it for us. Gentle reader you should know that the writer of this column does very little laundry. He has a live in maid. The truth is we wash more items now than back then but it takes so little of our time. In Calvertville, most kids and many adults wore the same outfit from the skin out all week or close to it.

Today laundry is not an all day task. It is not unusual for BW or me to do a load of laundry while we are watching television on Thursday evening. It is so simple that even I can do it. Aren't automatic washers and dryers wonderful laborsaving devices? And don't forget the electric iron that consummates the process. Ironing time has fallen off the chart compared with yesteryear.

When our girls, TW and TM, were growing up, they were exemplars of how people today wear an item once and then it goes into the laundry hamper. Then if they went out at night, they threw that outfit in the hamper. If they tried an outfit on and rejected it, it went into the hamper also. After all laundry was so easy.

Question: Why do we call the washer and dryer automatic? The truth is they both require human input before they function. If they were automatic, the washer would collect the filthy, fetid garments, fill with water, wash the clothing and then put them in the dryer. The dryer would dry the garments and place them on hangers or fold them. Then the automatic iron would press them and place them in the closet or drawer. Now that would be automatic. Back to the story.

We usually knew that we were going to have beans and cornbread for dinner and supper on Monday. It was easy and could be cooked while Mom did the laundry. While the laundry was bubbling and cooking in the washer, the beans were bubbling and cooking in the huge pot on the stove. On the farm we ate dinner at noon and supper in the evening, by the way. Does anyone know the meaning of the phrase, "By the Way?" Why do we use it and what is its derivation?

In the heat of the summer we would build a fire under the big black iron kettle out in the barnyard to heat the water. Brother and I had the job of keeping the fire stoked. If we let the fire go out, we would get stoked because that was analogous to stopping the assembly line in a factory. We did heat some water on the wood burning or coal burning stove or used water from the stove reservoir. However, such quantities of water were needed that in the summer time the house would get unbearably hot so we did it outside. Later when we got electricity, we heated the water on the stove. What a relief!

The wringer washer mom used was a tremendous leap forward from the scrub board or beating them on rocks. Every article, starting with light colors, was washed in the same water that was one millidegree from steam. I never did understand that Mom put bluing in the water to make the white items whiter. After the agitator did its work we used a dowel rod to fish the garments out of the lava water and fed them through the rubber rollers to squeeze the water out, the spin dry cycle. The next stop was a number 10 galvanized tub, the rinse cycle, and then back through the rollers.

Then a wet rag was used to wipe rust and dirt off the clothesline. Another tub was used to lug the leaden garments to the clothesline or the solar-powered dryer - the dry cycle. We had a-shaped and the new and improved clip clothespins. Garments were sun dried in the summer and frozen dry in the winter.

Overalls and work clothes were done last because they were the dirtiest and since clothes line space was critical they were hung on the fence. Rags were also in with the overalls and they were hung on the bushes since they had lowest status. That is the origin of the axiom, "That puts the rag on the bush" which means a task is finished.

Periodically BW sallies forth into the Valley of Laundromania to do battle with the diabolical Dirt Devil from the hostile Kingdom of Soilistan. The truth is she walks down the hall, flips some switches, adds soap and then watches TV while "May Tag" and "Ken Moore" do the laundry. I think she would give me up before she would give up her washer, dryer and iron.

Eeek! That's A Bug!

I had a first this week. It is late September, the weather is cool and the house temperature fell to the lower sixties. Well BW thought that was too cold for a mortal to exist so she thought that she would turn on the furnace. She moved the thermostat setting from off to auto and to heat and waited for the huff or puff sound from the furnace that indicates that the gas valve has allowed gas to enter the burn chamber, the pilot has ignited said gas, and heat is on the way. Well, much to our chagrin, there was no huff or puff and no heat. It is good, though, that it did not blow the house down either. I went to the furnace room and discovered that the pilot light was out.

Now I operate on a rather low tech threshold. If something doesn't work, I hit it with a hammer. If it still doesn't work I get a larger hammer. At this point of the story I believe that a joke is in order. Prepare to laugh boisterously. Get ready because here comes the joke — a humorous anecdote. A fellow was practicing skydiving. He bailed out of the plane and at the proper time pulled the ripcord to open the chute. Nothing. He pulled again. Nothing. He pulled everything that even looked like a ripcord. Nothing. The Grim Reaper was smiling in his face as he looked down and saw the ground coming up at him at Mach 9.

In desperation, he looked down and he saw a man coming upward. As they neared each other the parachutist yelled, "Do you know anything about parachutes?" The other man replied, "No, do you know anything about lighting the pilot light on a gas furnace?" A little gas humor for your reading pleasure.

As you might deduce from that story, I do not light pilot lights on gas stoves, furnaces or water heaters. I have no experience in that field and I value my life and those who live with me enough not to mess with it. I know one thing about gas — it will explode and burn. Enough said. Don't mess with it. Suffice it to say I did not go for my hammer in this instance. So who you gonna' call?

Reluctantly, while hugging my checkbook close to my heart, I called a company in Plainfield to check it out. The same day a repairman came to the door. Correction, it was a repairwoman. Correction, she is not a repairwoman, she is a furnace technician. Well excuse me. And therein lies my tale.

She was quite young, late 20s or early 30s. It seems that everyone is young to me any more. Unlike many male repairmen, excuse me, repairpersons, no technicians, who have large stomachs and low riding jeans, she was quite svelte and trim in her uniform. She wore her hair in a no nonsense ponytail with a few strands strategically dangling over her face. I know this a sexist remark but she was quite attractive; the best looking repairman who ever came to my house. So sue me.

I found out that she is the daughter-in-law of a teacher where I formerly worked. Don't hold that against her. Her fingernails were not long and painted. In fact they were cut almost to the quick because she works with her hands. She came in the house looking like Old Saint Nick with her tool bag packed with tools and stuff. It also looked like a giant canvas purse.

Her English and communication skills impressed me. And equal to that she was quite erudite and adept at diagnosing the cause of the problem. After a short time she stated that the gas valve was not working. It would not allow gas to flow to the heating chamber. She wrote an estimate and I reviewed it as if I knew what I was doing. She could have sold me a dog and I wouldn't have realized it until it barked for food. The amount of the estimate bit through my checkbook like sharp puppy teeth through your shirtsleeve. I then asked for time to get a second opinion. She thanked me and left.

Later in the day I called the company and authorized the repairs. Two days later she came back with the equipment and parts. She said hello, smiled and turned to her work. In just a few minutes she had the furnace operating.My testosterone level got the better of me and I had to ask if she knew how to repair a software problem on my computer and she couldn't. I asked her if she could repair my garage door opener or a battery powered screwdriver. She apologized and said that she could not repair any of those items. I smiled knowingly but I didn't tell her that I couldn't either.

My second genuine surprise came as we were setting the thermostat. She removed the cover and something fell to the floor. "What was that?" she asked. "I don't know," I replied. She reached down to retrieve the dark object and upon closer examination, discovered that it was a dead bug. "Eeek, that's a bug!" she yelped and threw it down. I found that to be incongruent with her occupation and abilities.

We chuckled and I said, "Women, may think they can get along without men on this planet, but that is a misnomer. Women will never be able to get along without men. We are the hunters, TV remote operators, reachers of high things and killers of bugs."

She laughed and said, "In that respect, I think you are right." I wrote a check and she was on her way.

The Little Blue Potty

(Warning: This article may not be suitable for reading by children under the age of two. Parental guidance is suggested.)

Most children are born with the necessary systems in place and most have the usual and customary capacity. However, for some inexplicable reason when children get in a car to go on vacation, or just around the block, the capacity of certain organs mysteriously shrinks to the size of a thimble. And, it seems that the words they say most frequently, once they begin to talk, are "Me gotta potty," "I haftto potty," or many times it is the Readers Digest version of "potty! potty! Potty!" When I heard those words wailed in a high pitched, desperate voice, I knew my job was to facilitate the completion of the act or clean up afterwards. Believe me the former is preferable over the latter although neither is on my top ten list of things I would like to do today.

Upon further reflection the most frequently heard expression in households where children are at the toilet training stage, is not said by the child, but by the parents. It becomes a mantra especially when the family is in the car traveling Route 66 trying to make Albuquerque before night. How many times have I heard, "Joshua, do you have to go potty?" It seems that no matter how often a parent inquires, the stock answer from Joshua, the projectile pooping/peeing machine, (PPM) is, "NO!" PPM then continues to play as if any bodily function was the last thing on his mind. Seconds or maybe nanoseconds later he begins to wail about potty, potty, potty, or, the odoriferous emanations from the vicinity of PPM is a dead giveaway as to why he does not have to go potty. He has already grunted a gift in his Garanimals. That takes me back a long way.

Early in my elementary school life the bodily functions became known as numbers 1 and 2. When I was in Calvertville grade school, we would hold up either one finger or two fingers and the teacher would know where we needed to go and why. She would grant us leave time from class accordingly. If you do not know what numbers 1 and 2 mean, stop reading this article now and seek counsel from a six year old. Now that I have joined the ranks of males who have more of their life behind them than in front of them, I can identify with that emergency feeling mostly concerning number 1. All retired men can identify with what I am alluding to. You never want to be too far from Ft. Necessity, do you? If you don't know what I am talking about here, stop reading and seek counsel from any old codger over the speed limit. Back to children.

When our two daughters (TW and TM) were quite young, we had a little blue potty. It was a plastic bowl with a fluted or flared top and a coffee-cup like handle on it. I believe it was once used as the receptacle in a wooden toilet training chair. When they were a bit past that stage we put it in the car and it became the portable potty or the LBP. It was housed under the front seat of the car and it went everywhere we went. It just didn't get out of the car very often except for cleaning and sanitizing. When the wail and cry went up about needing to go potty, BW would whip out the LBP and the deed could be completed at 60 miles per hour right there on the hump in the floor where the drive shaft went back to the rear axle.

Oh the times I have driven down the road, the air redolent with the essence of LBP. As soon as practical I would stop and BW would discretely empty the contents on the berm of the road. While the LBP was being dumped, sometimes the horn would sound attracting attention to the action. I never did understand how that happened. That is my story and I am sticking with it.

Later when they were a little older, we would stop on the side of the road open the front and back doors and place the LBP on the ground, and the deed would be discretely completed outside the car. However, as time passed the girls would be exceedingly reluctant to use the potty because they felt that people could see them. We tried to persuade them otherwise although we knew it was possibly true.

The most incommodious result, yes the pun is intended, of the scenario involving the LBP, was spillage. Many times a spillage of bodily fluids and other contributions would occur in the car. Believe me no oil tanker or chemical tanker spill could do more damage to the environment and ecosystem than the LBP spill. I can not count the times that for some reason the potty would be turned over in the car with the resulting spillage. It was hard to breathe. I had to roll the window down even in inclement weather. Sometimes when it did not get tumped over right away, the tension would be so high in the car that I would shriek, "Come on, get it over with. Kick it over now. I can't stand the suspense!"

If you see a car going down the road with the driver side window down even next winter in a snow storm or this summer in a rain storm, check it out and I'll bet my next pay check against yours, that you will find a LBP in that car and it will be turned upside down. However, you will also find an expression of relief on the face of the PPM.

BW Looks Like a Terrorist

BW, my wife, and a friend flew stand-by to Florida last month. Peggy's husband is a mechanic for the ATA ground and support equipment and he has a perquisite (perk) that gives them so many free tickets per year. When he retires they can fly anywhere, anytime. What a deal! Some restrictions apply. One day, Peggy and her son flew to Denver for lunch.

Peggy called on a whim last week and invited BW to fly to Florida. They threw some things into a carry-on bag for the two-day trip and they were off like a scalded dog.

We have not flown since the September 11 tragedy so we are inexperienced in the new screening procedures at Indy International. Don't be deceived, we are not world travelers by any stretch of spandex. We fly once, maybe twice a year. This was BW's first experience at the new requirements and she had an epiphany.

She only had one small carry on bag for the two-day trip. That small bag was her undoing. She like me, keeps certain items in the bag at all times so we don't have to pack them for visiting Audreyville, our granddaughter, vacations and overnight trips. It is just easier.

She placed her bag on the X-ray machine so they could get the inside story. Gongs sounded, people came running and hustled her to the side. They had found a weapon in her bag. It was a pair of sewing scissors in a sewing kit. They were about the size of her forefinger, but they were considered a weapon. She was given two options: take them back to the car or kiss them good-bye. They went into the trash container. Question: Why do we say a pair of scissors when there is only one. Why a pair of pantyhose but only one bra? I ponder about such things.

Now the security people were on her like a bad summer heat rash. She had to remove her shoes for hoof inspection. Then she had to raise her arms and turn around for visual inspection. That was not sufficient. She was also subjected to the wand scanner. They passed an electronic scanner over her body trying to detect any explosives or metal weapons. So far so good.

At this point BW was singing *Happy Trails to You.* Hold on to your Fruit of the Looms, she is a long way from boarding.

With that behind her, she began to think Florida and confidently put the bag on the belt the second time. Sirens sounded and she was roughed up and taken aside. This time they found a pair of, there is that phrase again, fingernail clippers deep within the bowels of the bag. They were a souvenir from Hershey, Pennsylvania, but she had the same options as before. They joined the scissors in the black hole of forget it. Now the suspicions that she was a terrorist hung in the air like a bad smell.

At last she was free to go again. The bag went onto the belt the third time. This time the National Guard scrambled a jet, a company of troops stormed the area and BW looked like she had told as many lies as O.J. told. Her bag was being tossed around like a Nerd at a biker rally in Sturgis, South Dakota.

This time they found a second pair of scissors inside her purse that was inside the bag. They were smaller than the first pair. Meanwhile Peggy was standing over on the side looking like a member of the Dillinger Gang trying to escape detection by Melvin Purvis. Same options. Same result.

They finally slunk onto the aircraft, feeling like Thelma and Louise at a revival meeting. After a three-hour flight they joined friends in Florida and spent two glorious days in the sun. Too soon they had to return to the airport for the return flight.

Security personnel were on high alert. The alert went out as soon as she stepped out of the car. Electronic messages raced through computer terminals, phone calls flew threw the lines to various offices and a series of hand and smoke signals were passed through the terminal. "She's back," they said. It was the mere tip of a long seam of guilt that snaked its way back through the garment that was their stand-by flight experience.

BW scanned her ticket and with a chuckle showed Peggy a huge "S" that was stamped on it. I think she is officially listed on Attorney General Ashcroft's suspected list of terrorists. She really got the inspection that time. Security was tighter than the lug nuts on a '53 Chevy pickup. Peggy stood over by the baggage stand and laughed — quietly. They stamped a huge "T" on BW's forehead and let her go.

I was blissfully unaware that I lived with a terrorist. Keeps me up at night, wondering.

Simon and Mary Ann Have A Confusing Summer

Simon and Mary Anne are from the old school. Truth be told they are out of the loop on many topics of the day. They have had their car so long that it now has to have bifocal headlights. Simon is courteous toward Mary Ann and other women. He still walks on the traffic side on the sidewalk. He opens the door for her and other women. He will also hold the door for men. He always allows her to go first through a door. In a restaurant she goes before him as they are directed toward a table. He says please and thank you when Mary Anne does something for him. She does likewise. When a woman enters the room and engages Simon he always stands, bows slightly and greets her courteously. He remains standing until she sits or moves away.

Mary Anne is courteous and friendly. If she were walking through the Gobi Desert by herself and belched she would say excuse me. She is a hugger and one who reaches out to others. Everyone feels warm, invited and included when she is near. She is concerned with the well being of others almost to a fault. In their long marriage, she has deferred to Simon in many aspects of their lives. It is not a patronizing attitude or one of second class citizenship. He in turn defers to her in many aspects of their lives. Thoughtfulness, courtesy and cordiality are support beams in the building that is their life.

They have had a confusing summer. They attended the high school graduation party of a great niece and gave her a practical gift. Remembering when their children went to college and how they needed practical items for everyday use, they purchased a brightly colored plastic bucket and filled it with shampoo, soaps, toothpaste, a toothbrush, a loofah, a fluffy bath towel, two wash clothes to match and other items. At the party they noticed that there were no other presents on the table, just envelopes that looked like congratulatory cards. They were puzzled thinking that maybe the gifts had been given earlier. After a suitable period of time they went on home.

Two days later Simon answered the doorbell to find the mother of the great niece. She was holding their gift. He invited her in but she declined and said, "I know that it has been awhile since you attended a graduation party and you probably aren't aware of how times have changed, but your gift is not very appropriate for today's graduate. College is so expensive that people today give money and most of them give at least $200. She handed him the bucket and said, "I'm sure you would like to correct this little faux pas." With that she turned and left.

They were invited to the wedding of their minister's daughter who looked a little rotund around her waist. They gave some fluffy towels, wash cloths, dish towels and a framed copy of the wedding invitation. At the wedding, the bridesmaids and others opened the few gifts. Again Simon and Mary Anne were confused. One of the bridesmaids sought them out and informed them that people were giving money toward the honeymoon the couple was taking in the Caribbean. "The towels are nice," she said, "but hardly appropriate since they had been living together for so long that they had those items anyway."

A month later it was announced that the couple was having a baby and that she was about six months pregnant. Simon and Mary Anne thought about baby gifts. They thought and thought and remembered about what they had received many years before and what their own children had gladly received. They are not very conversant with the concept of registering at various stores. So once again they thought practical and purchased several items to be used in personal hygiene of the baby such as oil, shampoo, wash cloths, bath towel and ointments for diaper rash. The present was unwrapped and displayed with others during the come and go shower. Imagine their chagrin when they overheard two people who did not know they had brought the gift say, "Who brought that stuff, The Clampetts? Do they live in a cave? Haven't they ever heard of registering for gifts?"

Now you see why Simon and Mary Anne have had a confusing summer.

Audrey at Eleven Months
Grampa Took A Nap Too

I warned readers several months ago in a column that I titled "It Is Payback Time," that since "Grampahood" was a long time in coming for me I would have to make up for lost time. You received fair warning that at any moment I could begin rhapsodizing about our preemie granddaughter Audrey. Unlike threats that the government must deal with concerning the Taliban and Osama Bin Laden, these will cause you no trauma.

Audrey is a dazzling blonde with the biggest blue eyes since Elizabeth Taylor. She has the power to stun you with her love ray and wriggle her way into your heart and lodge there. Her hair is getting longer and curlier each day. Many people have asked where she gets her blonde hair and blue eyes since both her daddy and mommy have black hair and dark eyes. Both her parents had blond hair when they were in their baby goathood days. BW also reminded everyone that I had blonde curly hair through high school and beyond. Then she drolly observed, "That was when he had hair." What a shot to the old solar plexus! That was cold and totally unnecessary. I still have green eyes, though.

Audrey is a singer. She sang several duets with her grammie last week. Each new one sounded similar to the last one but that is okay. They sounded a bit like Johnny One Note but her performance had Broadway written all over it. I can just see her name in lights. Her trademark sound reminds me of Fred Waring and the Pennsylvanians. If you remember that group you probably don't have a house payment anymore.

She is a laugher. She has a most pleasant personality like her Grampa Van. Laughter comes bubbling up from deep within her like cake batter pouring from a mixing bowl. When she smiles her face lights up the night like a dusk to dawn light. She can make you smile even if your feet are killing you.

However, she does get tired of entertaining everyone. When she gets drowsy she can look right through you into another dimension. With a couple of blinks of the eyes, she is gone to never never land. She sleeps most of the night and she has for some time now. It is not unusual for her to waste five hours at a time in uninterrupted snoozing. She is making up for earlier when her sleep patterns resembled network television programs. You know the kind. We tried to watch a two-hour movie recently and realized that there were nine minutes of movie followed by nine minutes of ads. You can set your clock for 30 minutes when she naps during the day. Remarkable. She could be a horologist — one who makes and repairs clocks.

You who are old enough can relate to this if you ever drove a team of horses. I remember that drivers would make a clicking or scritching noise that meant giddyup to the horses. Audrey makes that same clicking sound when prompted. She sounds like a cricket in the summer grass. She can also pop her lips like a small firecracker.

She cruises around furniture while holding on as her wobbly legs do their Ginger Rogers impression. She walks rapidly if someone holds her arms. In fact, she just may skip the crawling step if her parents let her. She is a leader since she is always in front of the one holding her arms. It is hard on backs but Audrey never tires. She reminds me a bit of the orangutan in the movie "Every Which Way But Loose." She is good at falling which is followed by massive puckering which is followed by wailing and gnashing of toofie. That lasts for a moment or two and then she is back at it.

She is in training for the Olympic gluttony team. She eats mandarin orange pieces, cheese, cantaloupe, cereal, baby food chicken and broccoli, veggie wheels, green beans, carrots, fruit juice, crackers and bread.

On Mothers' Day she was the center of attention at the Galt House in Louisville as two parents, four grandparents and one great grandmother doted on her. We took 870 pictures as she ate and entertained us. On the way home she went to sleep. When grampa got home he took a nap too. He is entitled. It is hard work being a Grampa.

Audrey Has Two Toofies!

Audrey Alert! Audrey Alert! I always warn readers when I feel an urge to write about our precious granddaughter. Her name is Audrey Grace Carter. "Her Grace" came to visit us this past weekend. Her dad calls her that because she acts like a Queen of royalty when she demands attention. She was thoughtful enough to bring her mother Sharla and her father Todd with her to help drive the car.

Audrey is ten months old and growing like a weed. I remember the first time I saw her she was a red, wrinkled, tiny doll-like bit of protoplasm. She looked like a Barbie Doll that had put on a little weight. Todd and Sharla called her "Little Bit."

She was in Norton Hospital in Louisville in an isolette unit that was heated and had an adjustable bed. A snappy knit cap covered her head and her body was swaddled in so many wrapping she looked like she was in a flannel grocery bag. She also had a tube inserted through her nose and down to her stomach. I hurt when I looked at her. Even though it was for her good and she could not live without it, it made my stomach tighten and my eyes mist a bit to see her.

She weighed 35 ounces at birth and just a few days later she weighed an astounding 30 ounces. From that day to this she has been on an uphill climb and now weighs a strapping, muscular 15 pounds which is within four to five pounds of what a full-term baby would normally weigh. She is eating cereal, meat, veggies and other items that mom and dad sneak to her from their plates. It is interesting to watch her pick up a piece of green bean, exam it, place it in her mouth, investigate it with her tongue and then gum it. She has two toofies on the bottom but they are just breaking through. She is on the way to looking like Br'er Rabbit. She has discovered that she likes food from her mommie and daddie's plate. So, being quite astute, they put her food on their plates and presto, she thinks, "What a deal, they eat the same thing that I do."

I remember playing games as a child. One game required the participant to be blindfolded and taken to a place and he would have to determine where he was. Or he had to guess what was going on. Today if you were to blindfold me and lead me to a place and I could sense that there were people, and I could smell Cheerios, I would know that I was in a church building. Cheerios is the food of choice for mothers and babies in church. All babies like Cheerios. So does Audrey. She can pick them up and place them in her mouth with about 50% accuracy on the first try.

She sits up with no help. Just about a month ago she could not sit without assistance and she could not hold her head still. She looked like a bobble head doll that the Pacers would give away at half time. Maybe she was bobbin' to her own beat. She was with it, if you know what I mean.

She has progressed to the point that she can stand up briefly and is she tickled with herself. She thinks that she is the first baby to ever accomplish that trick. Truth be known, she is the only baby she is aware of to achieve that feat. She plays and sings to herself and to us. She also has a propensity to scream. It is a primal expression of life. It can become a little annoying at times, however. No, it is a whole lot annoying.

She reaches for toys and items that interest her. She grasps the plastic donuts from the stackable rings and manipulates them to her own pleasure. Typical of all babies she chews, hugs, licks and throws them.

We are thinking that Audrey is going to go from sitting, to standing to walking and skip crawling all together. She has very strong legs and walks with **much** assistance. She reminds me of a spastic slinky toy.

Audrey is a nuzzler. I nuzzled her nose with mine. She stuck her little nose out and wanted to do it again, and again, and again. Of course I hated to do it but it is my duty as a grandfather. One thing about babies, if you don't want to do something ad infinitum, don't teach them to do it.

She has a cheerful disposition. She takes after her Grandpa Van in that regard. She communicates with grunts, chirps, loud cries, smiles and a devilish grin. Down right irresistible. She is among the top three cutest and most precious babies every born.

One final note, my Indiana Hoosiers made a run at the NCAA title this year all because Audrey has an IU cheerleader outfit. Enough said about that.

When You're Happy The Years Fall Away

Last Sunday was a typical hot and humid July day. A cold front dashed across the state in early afternoon bringing a bit of rain and a declivity of both temperature and humidity. Clouds hurried across the sky like clumps of people looking for festival symphony seating at Conner Prairie. I thought about Angie and Stephen who were preparing for an outdoor wedding at 6:30 that evening.

At the appointed time we were seated on the lawn of a conference and banquet center set on the immaculate grounds of a stately old manor house in a picturesque small town. The weather was perfect. A breeze stirred the tree leaves and the surrounding hedges. Sunlight streamed gently through the trees casting fingers of shadows as evening steadily marched toward us. The air was electric with anticipation. The gentle sounds of conversation and quiet laughter mingled with the lilting sounds of classical music and floated softly to my ears on the zephyr's breath.

Birds sang in the bridal chorus. Squirrels looked down from their lofty homes in the massive trees and wondered what we were doing. Babies giggled and cooed. The teenage girls made mental notes for their own weddings. Older couples were lost in reverie of times gone by. The cool breeze carried with it the hope of the future and the excitement to come. The invigorating fresh air was energizing.

Lights twinkled on the arches that adorned the temporary altar. The air was redolent with the pungent aroma of crushed grass under our feet. The trees waved their branches in thransonical celebration and approval.

Then the mood shifted and attention was riveted on the bridal party as the mothers were seated and the ceremony began. The parents were noticeably happy with the choices their children had made. The groom and groomsmen took their places. The bridesmaids took their places and the flower girl and ring bearer entered. And then everyone stood in rapt expectation as the bride and her father elegantly entered the ceremony treading ever so lightly on the white cloth road of anticipation that at its end would change their lives forever. It was a warm and tender moment. A smile nudged its way onto my face as my thoughts carried me back to the moments when I walked with my daughters down the same path. At such a time a father's heart needs a temporary pacemaker.

The wedding ceremony was short and elegant. The bride was radiant in white and lace. Her face was beatific with love and expectation. The elegantly attired groom exuded confidence and great love for his bride. Their eyes sparkled with quintessential ardor and their faces glowed with anticipation. They radiated ecstasy and the expectation of a long life transfused with daily megadoses of adoration, affection and devotion. The vows were given in beautiful and enthusiastic tones. Rings were exchanged with vows of eternal commitment. After the reception where a sumptuous banquet was served, the couple rode away on clouds of love for a honeymoon in Hawaii.

As I marinated in the ambiance of the evening, I felt the support and love that surrounded that young couple. Plates of well wishes were served up to them and I tasted the ambrosia of joy. My mind took me on a journey through time. I was on a sleek, jet-powered vessel that thrust upstream on the river of time through the challenging rapids of fear and the languid pools of joy, through the sun of happiness and shadows of doubt to a place long ago and far away.

I stood in a house on a cold February evening and watched another wedding. A friend played the piano and sang some songs. The young starry-eyed couple stood before their friends and family, stated vows and exchanged rings. Cake and punch were served. Then they rode on the arms of love into the winter winds and launched themselves into the state of matrimony. After spending two or three days in Martinsville and Indianapolis they rented an apartment in Indy and began their journey down the road of life.

That was over eight lustrums ago and I remember as if it were yesterday. Where has the time gone? In the words of a song, "Fall away, fall away, when you're happy the years fall away. When you're blue the days go by a draggin', but when you're happy the years fall away."

In the year 2045 Angie and Stephen will attend the wedding of a child, a grandchild or a friend and they will be swept away on the wings of nostalgia and remember this day as the day their lives truly began.

Weddings trigger emotions and release a torrent of memories. They also extend hope unto the next generation and to generations to come. That is why I attend.

It's Gone!

It is gone. Market Square Arena was imploded Sunday in Indianapolis. It made the national news and immediately went into reruns every few minutes on every TV in Indiana. News teams in Indy were there to film the demolition and to talk incessantly about it. The very people who asked that the public not come downtown to witness the event were all there witnessing the event.

Mother Teresa and Lady Diana died on the same weekend. Mother Teresa, noble, selfless, revered, honorable and venerated received minimal notice while Lady Diana was deified by the media for months. Johnny Russell, country music songwriter and singer died the same week as Mr. Nashville, Chet Atkins, and he was barely noticed. Bad timing.

It is gone. Another great structure was imploded last week and received no media coverage and it was sad. Implosion is too strong a word. It was pushed over by a huge excavator. The Calvertville store is a pile of rubble now just like Market Square Arena. It was difficult to see the icon of my past in that state. Memories flooded through my mind as I sorted through my mental scrapbook.

The store sat on the banks of the mighty Goose Creek on a small piece of ground near the Baptist Church and across the road from the feed mill. My earliest memories of the store were during the time when Mr. and Mrs. Ralph Martindale operated it and the feed mill. They had two children, Marilyn and Gary. I talked to Marilyn in June of 2001 at the Worthington Alumni Banquet. Then the Crites family operated the store. I can still see the store as it was. Women would produce a list and the clerk would flit throughout the store to get the items.

One bitterly cold winter day Bill Crites came into the store and stood by the potbellied stove to get warm. He was a young man and the older men kidded him about being cold. He said that he wasn't cold at all and showed us what he was wearing. He unzipped his coat and then began to unbutton his sweaters. He unbuttoned one then another and another and another. I remember him unbuttoning at least 12 sweaters. That is my story and I am sticking to it.

Once or twice a week the men of the community would gather at the store and gasconade — swap lies, tell tall tales and talk. It seems that when the men would gather Roy would frequently take center stage and bore the group with wearisome tales of his illnesses. I can still see the men rolling their eyes as he droned on and on.

One morning Brownie Neil came into the store and bought a bottle of coke and two glazed doughnuts. "What have you been up to," Ralph queried. Brownie said, "I've been out in the woods all day buying lumber." I thought, it isn't even noon yet why did he say he had been in the woods all day.

I thought about the time that my brother and I were taking corn to the feed mill to make into hog and chicken feed. I jumped off the trailer and grabbed some crab apples where Ray and Clara Brown lived. When I tried to get back on the trailer I fell and was dragged. Brother heard my cries and stopped. When we arrived at the store, Ralph took me into his house and patched up my wounds and called my mom.

On Friday nights we enjoyed free movies at the store. The movies were projected on the East wall of the store and people watched from the parking lot that was shared with the Baptist church. That brought shoppers to the store and provided entertainment for people who lived in isolation from the world.

Clyde Flory was our mailman forever. He would stop and eat his lunch near our house then go to the store and eat again. No wonder he became so fat.

I remember the salt fish barrel. Cheese came in a huge wheel. Ralph would cut off what you wanted. Paper sacks were unknown to us so he would tear off an appropriate length of brown paper from a huge roll, wrap the cheese and tie it with white string.

Gasoline was sold from two hand operated Standard Oil pumps. They had beautiful glass globes on top of a glass cylinder. Gas was hand pumped from the underground tank into the glass cylinder that had markings on the side like a measuring cup. Gravity then dispensed the gas through a hose to your vehicle.

The same person that pumped gas, wrapped cheese, checked oil, measured the brown sugar and packaged groceries would then cut meat. The board of health would close the place in a minute today.

For years Otto Baker was a mechanic at the two-bay garage on the West side of the building. If he couldn't fix it, throw it away. That is how good he was.

Several times I remember Dad backing the car under the porch to put on tire chains to get over the ice and snow covered hill that is between our house and the store.

How I would love to go into the store, get a coke from the cold water in the pop machine then get a bag of peanuts, pay Ralph a dime for both and go out on the porch. There I would sit on a nail keg, pour the nuts into the bottle and take a long refreshing swig. It doesn't get any better than that. But I will never be able to do that ever again because it is gone.

The Trunk Slammed Shut and Jill Was in Trouble!

Jill was going to the 20th reunion of her graduation from Verde College. Her husband was going to care for their children while she immersed herself in a nostalgic campus weekend, steeped her psyche in memories and wandered through the hills of reverie.

Jill decided to drive the ten-hour trip. She liked to drive and she would be by herself for the first time in a long time. Her family consumed much of her time and energy so this was going to be a respite for her. She anticipated seeing her old college friends and reliving the good old carefree college days. Her reverie took her down memory lane and she thought about the excitement of registration, moving in, pulling all nighters, football games, singing in the choir, working in student government and how she and her friends stayed up all night giggling and gabbing about everything and nothing. Life was so simple then. The only person she was responsible for was herself.

She could hardly wait to revisit old flames and the hangouts that were an integral part of their lives in the days when they knew everything and nothing but were blissfully unaware. She wanted to get a pizza at Antonio's, hang out at the union building, find her old dorm room and then visit the sorority house where she lived for three years.

She was flying down the Interstate enjoying the solitude when she stopped at a rest park. Being prudent she locked her valuables including her purse in the trunk of the car but she kept her key ring. After a visit to Ft. Necessity and doing some power walking to restore her energy, she opened the trunk, dropped the keys into her purse, found a sack of snacks and closed the trunk. As the sound of the closing trunk resonated through the chasms of her mind, she realized what she had done. It all happened in an "Ohnosecond" — the incredibly short period of time that it takes to realize that you have done something stupid. The keys and her purse were now locked in the trunk but she had her cheese crackers.

After a few minutes of anguish, she reasoned that all she had to do was call the road service number for Club Auto that was on the back window of the car. No problem. Problem! She had no money. Guess where it was!

Swallowing her pride she bummed a couple of quarters. Club Auto promised that a service person would arrive soon. She waited 45 minutes. She bummed more quarters and called again. Club Auto was astonished that no one showed up and promised to send someone else. She waited another hour. The ten minute rest stop had now extended to two hours plus. She was frustrated. Desperation was entering the parking lot of her mind.

Finally, Max arrived in his service truck. On the door was his motto *Don't Cuss, Call Us*. Within a few seconds he used a "J Bar" and opened the car door. Smiling broadly he said, "Well, little lady, I reckon you are ready to go." "But you don't understand," Jill moaned, "my purse and keys are locked in the trunk. I still can't drive without my keys." "Well, that is a new ball game," Max said, "No one told me that I had to get into the trunk."

Max looked in the back seat. "You usta could pull the back seat up or down and get into the trunk that way. No such luck on cars nowadays," he said. Desperation pulled in and parked right beside Jill's car.

"You must do something," she whined at Max, "I'm already late to my college reunion. "Well," Max protested, "you gotta' have a key to get into a trunk, there ain't no other way short of breaking in, and I ain't got no key." "I could call a locksmith or a dealer but I don't know how long it would take to get somebody here."

"No, no," Jill protested, "there must be something you can do!" Max scratched his chin, looked down, kicked the curb and said, "I could drill out the lock and get in if you don't mind me messing up your lock." "Do it," Jill urged.

Max rummaged around and pulled out his cordless drill from his massive toolbox. Within a few minutes he had drilled out the lock mechanism and popped the trunk lid open. With a cheer, Jill came up from the Pit of Despair to the Plains of Joy. She was on her way. Watch out Verde, here I come.

She didn't make quite the impression she wanted to at Verde College. It is hard to be sophisticated, debonair and cool when your bouncing trunk lid is held shut with a bright red and yellow striped bungee cord.

I Have Had it Up to Here and Beyond With Cell Phones

I have had it up to here and beyond with cellular phones. Gentle reader, please know that the writer whose thoughts you are reading is an old Curmudgeon, a Geezer or to put it more crudely an Ancient Flatulator. He does not own or use a cell phone. I enjoy being out of touch sometimes. I have concluded that only those living in cells should use cell phones. My grievance is that many people today are so inconsiderate and rude when using their cellular phones.

Cell phones are the next generation of telephones. Before the invention of the cell phone, the regular telephone was the most intrusive device ever conceived by mind of man. When the phone rings, all activity stops and someone somewhere else suddenly is elevated to priority status over the here and now. I recently listed the other communication devices that are "must haves" to so many people and they march along in a company with the telephone. Remember the extra long cord, digital phones, pagers, beepers, answering machines, cordless phones, caller I.D., call waiting and instant redial. The outrageous aspect of this communication explosion is that Ameritech and the other "techs", Mamma Bell, and Tinker Bell race to the bank every day with more and more of your money. And they don't even use a gun to get it. Now let us return to my rampage — the cell phone.

Just prior to my retirement from public education I was conducting a seminar for teachers. During the activities of the seminar two of those present received calls. The nature of the calls was irrelevant and trite because we heard the conversation of the teachers. It was just insipid and banal chatter.

Recently I was serving communion during worship service. As I approached a man to serve him, his cell phone rang. During the worship service! Needless to say that was a major disruption to the worship time that we were engaged in. He fumbled, stumbled and mumbled several things into the phone. It was more meaningless chatter and drivel.

A short time ago BW and I accompanied another couple to pay our respects to dear friends in the death of her grandmother. As we rode in the car the man who was driving talked on his cell phone twice. On the way home he held two more conversations with someone else somewhere else. Since we did not have time to eat before we went, we stopped to eat at a restaurant. While we were eating and socializing he placed three calls and received two more. I allowed myself to become acrimonious, that is 30 miles beyond mad. I was seething. Obviously others in some other place were more important or convivial than I was. I just shut down socially.

I don't have to discuss the use of cell phones at social gatherings, while driving vehicles, sitting in meetings, restaurants and other times. Schools forbid cell phone use or students would spend the entire day talking to other students in other classrooms.

One Sunday afternoon I was rehearsing with a group of singers from our church in preparation for a special worship. During the rehearsal three women had to take phone calls from unknown people. The message that such people are conveying is that anyone anywhere is more interesting, entertaining or important than anyone here is. How utterly rude and discourteous.

I am not a prophet or the son of a prophet but I foresee the future when everyone will have their own personal communicating device and there will be no face to face conversations because everyone will be talking to someone else in some other location. People will still be in a group, but they will all be communicating to someone else in another location. How awful. How dreadful.

Now what? I just recently started a company called Goose Creek Communications, Ink. Our mission is to research and develop the penultimate communication device. Our laboratories are developing an implant called a FACIT (Futuristic Amplified Communicative Incessant Talking device). The device will be implanted behind the ear, in the cheek or temple. A sensor will be run through the inside of the mouth and terminate near the larynx to transmit the sound of the voice. A sensor will be connected to the tympani membrane in the ear to collect sounds and transmit them to the brain for decoding. A receiving and sending antenna will be implanted just under the skin around the top of the head like a car antenna embedded in the rear window. It can also be imbedded just under the skin on the arm that can be raised or lowered to improve reception. The FACIT is planned for production in time for sale at Christmas.

I have visions of sugarplums and of people lined up at Implants R Us, clamoring for the FACIT to be installed like a garage door opener. One thing for sure, I will be smiling like a TV evangelist when FACIT hits the market place. Look for it at Sprawl-Mart, Target and other big box stores everywhere. If you can't beat them, join them.

Julie Does Not Live In New York City

Large cities are simultaneously intriguing and threatening. They are intriguing because of all of the people who live together, huddled in masses like cattle seeking the shade of a small tree on a hot day. Opportunities as well as disappointments abound in large cities. As the song says you can be riding high in April and shot down in May because your life is held in the bony hands of the power brokers. You can live on Opportunity Boulevard and in Heartbreak Hotel in the same year. In the parade of life you can be on the trophy winning float waving to the crowds or you can be wheeling the cart and sweeping up the used hay behind the horse patrol.

Large cities are threatening. So many people in large cities appear to be in a hurry as they bustle along the streets. They are rude and discourteous because they feel that their time is wasted by rubes like me that are not in the flow of things. It has been my experience that drivers everywhere and especially in large cities are not very tolerant and exhibit miniscule bits of patience toward tourists when they slow down or fumble around the streets and thoroughfares searching for an elusive address. They make obscene gestures, blast their air horns, yell and gesticulate and then blow by while you struggle. It is especially egregious at rush hour or anytime by cab drivers and drivers of commercial vehicles or 18-wheelers and other huge trucks. Many of them drive as if they are the advance man for Forrest Lawn.

I am concerned in large cities because of the possibility of being caught on Holdup Street. On that street bad people might force me to dance the dance of fear while they steal everything except my fruit of the looms. Large cities are so anonymous and impersonal. It seems that everyone lives on Self Absorbed Boulevard and works in the Me-First Building.

I expressed those fears and concerns to Julie who has lived in New York City for about 20 years. She said, "I don't live in New York City. No one does. I live in Queens. Actually I live in a neighborhood called Astoria." She went on to share some anecdotes about her life there.

One day Julie went to an ATM machine withdrew $200, stuffed it into her pocket and went on her way. Later she reached into her pocket and discovered that the money was not there. Now $200 may not be much to you but Julie considers it a sizeable sum. She began a quest by backtracking where she had been as she searched every nook and cranny. She rummaged through her purse and every pocket. Her search was an exercise in futility.

She went on to work and the thoughts of the lost money edged into her consciousness throughout the day. It loomed over her lunch like a dark cloud. After work she trudged home and glumly turned the key in the lock and with downcast spirit entered her apartment.

Half-heartedly she glanced at her phone and noticed the blinking red message light. The message said "come to the grocery store down the block and talk to Dominick, he has something for you." She hurried down the street and talked to Dominick who gave her the $200. He explained that a couple had found the money on the sidewalk near the ATM. Julie's receipt was with it and it had her name and address on it. They brought it to Dominick who knows Julie. How refreshing! Maybe I am wrong about some big city dwellers.

One winter day Julie slipped and injured her leg. The doctor put a heavy walking cast on it. Unfortunately it was still quite painful. It was after dark when Julie struggled into her apartment and plopped into a chair. She had not eaten dinner.

On a whim, she called the delicatessen down the street, explained her predicament and inquired if perhaps they would deliver. She explained to Ben, the owner, who she was and he said, "I know who you are. You come in here frequently." He assured her that he would bring her the items she wanted. He then asked if she needed anything else? She hurriedly provided a short list of food items that she would need over the next few days. Ben went to the grocery store and within thirty minutes delivered the groceries and the deli items to Julie's door. And I thought that New Yorkers did not care about others. Perhaps I need a bit of an attitude adjustment.

After the horrible tragedy visited on the World Trade Center last week, I saw a new side of the people who live there. They obviously care for each other and will exert Herculean efforts to assist people in need. Maybe big cities are not so bad after all.

Penny's Free Bubble Gum Didn't Taste So Good After That!

Neighborhood stores of the past seemed to fit a pattern. They usually had gas pumps outside on the drive and a carport over the entrance. The front wall was mostly glass. They all had a screen door with Tastee or Bunny bread ads painted on the screen wire. The side walls had shelves all the way to the ceiling. Some had display cases in the front with the cash register. The refrigerated meat case was in the back and most had a pot bellied stove. The front display case usually contained candy, gum, and notions. They had a large roll of brown paper and a ball of white string to wrap purchases. Of course there was the red metal pop case with a cold water reservoir to cool the six-ounce soda pop. I remember Bob and Gayles Regal Store, Solidays, Tates, Diamond Point, Little Mexico, Flory's Store, Noel and Terrells, Noel and Franklin, Moore's Store and Border's IGA in my home town.

Penny frequented Flory's Store. She lived nearby. The store was an enchanting place where forbidden fruit hung from branches all over the store. The siren song was so strong that Penny wanted everything in the store but she was just a little kid and she had no money. She would go in and talk to Ollie.

The most seductive area was the candy counter. There were hundreds of confectionery items of sweet tantalizing deliciousness inside that glass-enclosed vault. Her mouth would water every time she passed it. The sweet ambrosia beckoned to her. Her taste buds longed for sweetness. She did not have a sweet tooth she had 32 of them.

One day she entered Flory's Store and slowly passed the candy window rubbing her fingers along the glass. She looked up and saw a sign that said, "Free - Take one." She couldn't believe her eyes. She looked, then looked again and looked a third time. The sign still said, "Free - Take

159

one." It was beside the Fleer's Bubble gum display. Fleer's gum was packaged in small cakes of pink rubberized material with creases to segment the gum into three portions. It also had a light coating of sweet white powder on the outside.

Penny was delighted. What a wonderful kismet; a serendipity! To you who are still learning that means a sudden unexpected pleasure. Enthralled by her sudden good fortune, she reached into the display and took a piece. She hurried out under the carport and popped the sweet, pink globule into her mouth. She chewed rapidly to get the flavor flowing and to prepare for a bubble extravaganza.

She skipped down the street humming a happy tune and blowing bubbles on her way home. As she came into the yard she chirped, "Hi daddy," and popped a large nose covering bubble. "Penny," he asked, "where did you get the bubble gum?" "At Ollie's store," she gleefully responded. Suddenly her dad became angry. Penny did not know why. He tore a switch off a nearby tree and swatted her behind. "Let's go to the store," he said angrily. Together they marched the two blocks to the store while Penny was served some elm tree tea along the way. The bubble gum lost its flavor and became hard as a rock.

The screen door slammed behind them. "Ollie," Penny's dad said, "I am sorry and embarrassed to tell you that my daughter stole some gum from you." Ollie looked surprised. "What? I can't believe it," he blurted, "she is such a fine girl!"

"Yes, she did. Penny tell Ollie what you did and apologize," her dad demanded.

Tearfully, Penny pointed to the little sign, "The sign says that it is free and to take one, so I took a piece."

Ollie looked. "I am sorry," he said, "that sign is for the handbills that are beside the bubble gum."

"I see," Penny's dad said, "but you should not have taken that bubble gum without asking Ollie. You don't take anything unless you pay for it. Do you understand? That isn't right!"

"Yes, daddy," Penny replied, "I am sorry, Ollie."

"Ollie," her dad said, "Penny will be in your store every day for the next week and she will sweep the floor to pay for that gum and to learn her lesson." With that, he shook Ollie's hand, put his arm around Penny and they walked back home in dead silence.

For the next week, Penny dutifully swept the store for Ollie. Ollie felt so badly about the sign that he gave her a bottle of pop and a candy bar every day. Ollie and Penny remained friends and Penny never took anything again, even if it said free.

That's Almost 30!

Karen was born in Oklahoma but she grew up in West Texas. She has an open personality, gentle manner and a smile bigger than Alaska. She was the youngest in a family of four girls in a household with no father figure. For reasons unknown to me her biological father hit the bricks when she was quite young.

Karen's mother moved the family to Austin, Texas, to be closer to her family. She frequently worked two jobs to keep the wolf from the door. As soon as the girls were old enough they also worked to ease the financial burden. In spite of their deprivations the family was bright and cheerful. They were deeply religious because of the model that their mother set. Their church family was a vital part of their everyday lives.

Karen had shining blonde hair that danced in the wind like gossamer wings. Her eyes were limpid pools of blue that sparkled like sunlight on icicles. Her smile was bigger than all outside. She had an outgoing personality and her disposition was sunny and as bright as a day of July sunshine. She was a good student. You would want all of your students to emulate her.

When she was a young teen her two older sisters were already married. One day she asked her oldest brother-in-law his age. He said, "I'm 27 years old." To which Karen blurted out, "That's almost 30!" Karen was not much of a blurter but she couldn't help it that time. Everyone had a laugh. Al, the brother-in-law, laughed as heartily as anyone but he did not forget.

Karen graduated from high school and Abilene Christian University and gained a degree in Home Economics. She was a high school teacher for a time. During the time she was in the university, she met a soldier who was a gentleman and more handsome than Harrison Ford. He was stationed at an Army base in Texas. After a suitable time, they married when he was on a three-day pass.

He later served in Vietnam and was badly wounded to the extent that one of his legs was amputated. They remained happily married. The years passed and Karen approached the Big Three Zero. She was a busy homemaker with two young sons and a happy and productive life. She knew that her 30th birthday was peeking in the window but she, like many, pushed it to the background of her consciousness and engaged in her daily activities.

One day the doorbell jangled and yanked her back to reality. The local florist was delivering a huge box of flowers with a card that read, "Welcome to Old Age." She whipped the box open to find 30 beautiful flowers — spray painted black. Immediately she suspected her husband but he vehemently denied responsibility. Her attention then turned to her brothers-in-law.

She called the florist and inquired about the sender. The florist said that she was bound to secrecy under penalty of severe consequences. "Tell me this," Karen asked, "Does the person live east of the Mississippi River or West of the Mississippi River?" The florist stammered, hemmed and hawed, coughed a few times and then quietly said, "I can not reveal the person's name but the person does not live east of the river." Instantly Karen knew that it was Al, the brother-in-law about whom she remarked many years earlier that he was "nearly 30." The gauntlet had been thrown down and the battle was on.

When Al was 50 Karen sent the same flowers to his home. They were a bit bedraggled and frazzled but the message was sent and received. When Karen was 40 the same flowers were delivered back to her house. Now they were really looking sad. However, the message rang loudly and clearly throughout the land.

Then when Al was 60, UPS delivered the flowers again. What do you suppose happened when Karen was 50? Correct. The door bell rang and to no one's amazement, the FedEx man held a beat up box containing the remnants of those black flowers now some twenty years old and with frequent flier miles attached.

Today the bits and pieces of those flowers stand ensconced in a vase at the top of the stairs in Karen's home. And that is where they will remain. Before Al reached another milestone, Karen lost her long battle with cancer. Any young girl today seeking a role model to pattern her life after as a woman, wife and mother, need look no further than Karen.

I hate To Shave!

"I wish I was old enough to shave," I would say to Dad as he performed his daily ablutions at the old kitchen sink by the door. I was barely as tall as the sink and not half as tall as my dad. The sink he used had no way to get water into it except that which was poured from some vessel. This was so long ago that we did not have running water in the house.

Dad would dip water out of the reservoir on the end of the stove or pour some out of the teakettle that resided permanently on the stove. He would put the water in an enamel pan and place it in the sink. Then he would take his shaving mug that held the soap and brush, dip the brush in the hot water and swirl it around in the mug to make lather. Just before he lathered his face he would splash the hot water on his beard. The next step was to apply the lather-filled horsehair brush to his face and upper lip. How I wanted to lather my face. Sometimes he would touch my nose or chin with the brush. The soap was smooth and creamy and felt so good. I still remember the clean, crisp manly aroma of Williams Shaving Soap. Then Dad would scrape his whiskers off with his trusty single edged Gillette Razor.

Sometimes he would lather my face and let me shave. Of course he removed the blade first but I didn't care. It felt great to do manly things. In those prehistoric days a blade would only be good for a few shaves and then it would become so dull and rusted that it had to be discarded. Shaving took great strides when the two-edged blade was introduced. It made no difference to me then because I shaved without a blade.

I remember the straight edge razor that required a strap to keep it sharp. I have fond memories of Bill Dixon and others stropping the straight edge to hone its sharpness. In the 60's a new kind of blade was introduced that was sharper and lasted much longer. I recall sitting in the Savage Barbershop in Tipton, Indiana and hearing conversations about the new stainless steel blade and how long it lasted. Glory it was good. An aside — it was the Savage barbershop because the brothers Savage operated it not because of the treatment you received.

Electric shavers became popular years ago. The first ones were wind up spring driven models developed for use in Antarctica. The first ones had a flat face or edge and then rotary heads were introduced. Electric and battery power replaced the spring driven kind. Today, you can buy a battery-powered razor that dispenses shaving cream and use it while you are showering.

I have used an electric shaver for many years. Recently I returned to lather and blades. I use the three-blade Mach 3 by Gillette. It has a cartridge with three blades in it and it lasts a long, long time. I'm not convinced as the ads say that it shaves you closer. They will tell you anything to sell a product. I have also discovered that any cheap lather will work. I have used shaving soap with a brush, gel applied with the hands, paste like toothpaste, aerosol lather, lather that is heated in the can and now I am back to the aerosol can. I recommend Barbasol.

A thought has occurred to me. Why don't men use Nair? I see it advertised for women! I would like to skip shaving for days or weeks like they say for women's legs. Maybe it is too girly! Real men shave every day.

For years when men went to the barbershop men like Bill Dixon and Mort Trent shaved your neck after the cut. No More. I wonder why. I realized recently that male barbers are on the endangered species list. More and more women are moving in and men are moving out. For the last 14 years I have frequented a barbershop that has one man, the owner, and he employs three women for the other chairs. Ninety-nine times out of a hundred a woman cuts my hair. Actually I only get about six or seven haircuts per year. There is a great turnover in the women, but Bob has always been there.

Shaving does not hold the enchantment that it did to a rag-a-muffin boy watching his dad shave many years ago. Today, I hate to shave.

Robert Will Forever be 19 Years Old

The battered marine footlocker sat unnoticed in the back closet of the old house on Dayton Street. It was covered with an oilcloth kitchen tablecloth. It was discovered in 1975 when Harold Taylor, the executor and Tim Crocker, auctioneer, were preparing for the sale to close the estate of Kenneth Ronan.

The footlocker was military issue and quite old. The hinges were rusted and they complained when the lid was opened. The latch was off of one side. It was scratched and dented because it had been to the Pacific and back. It was dust covered and many spiders had made their webs on every available surface. Harold opened the lid and was greeted with the musty smell so prevalent in trunks and boxes that have remained closed for many years.

The enclosed artifacts summarized several lives. Near the top was a black and white picture of a lovely young bride who had the spirit of life in her eyes. She was lovely and resplendent in her wedding gown. On the back was inscribed My Clara 1923.

Next to it was a picture of a young man with a strong chin wearing a dark suit and an ill-fitting white shirt and tie. His hair was slicked down and combed straight back. He had a determined and confident look in his eyes. Hope and determination exuded in his gaze. The world lay before him and was there for the taking. On the back was the name Kenneth Ronan, 1923. A third picture was a wedding picture of Clara and Kenneth.

Just under the pictures was their marriage license dated September 4, 1923. The names were scribed in beautiful calligraphy as Kenneth Ronan and Clara Randle. They were married by Rev. Jonathan Finbar in Clarksville.

Included with the license was a lace handkerchief and a Bible used in the wedding. A birth certificate was just under the license announcing the birth of Robert Ronan in

1924. Scattered helter-skelter through the locker, were mementos of Robert's life. There were pictures of a chubby, bright-eyed baby and of a young child going off to school in the first grade. On the back of the picture was inscribed "Our Robert - first day of school." There were some report cards that revealed that Robert had some good subjects and good years and some not so good. Baby shoes, socks and a couple of diapers were included. A few toys were also included in the mementos. Evidently he liked baseball because his mildewed mitt and a frayed baseball lay in the bottom.

Enshrined with the many historical objects was a blue velvet covered high school diploma issued to Robert in 1942. There was also a yearbook embossed with the title "The Oracle", 1942. The pages had turned brown on the edges and were tattered and stained with the oil of many inquiring fingers. It had been opened and read many times. Many of Robert's classmates had written in it and signed their names. Included with the yearbook were pictures of the '42 prom, tickets to the dance and a crumbled and dried boutonnière. Knowing smiles worked their way across the faces of Harold and Tim.

Their minds turned somber as they found a picture of a smiling young man of 19 years in a U.S. Marine dress blue uniform. They also found induction papers, dog tags, a boot camp graduation picture and a newspaper article. As they lifted the items some rusty razor blades and a marine issue safety razor tumbled out. There were several letters from Robert to his parents and a web belt. Under all of that regalia was a neatly folded U.S. Flag.

With the flag was a telegram from the War Department, U.S. Marine Corp, Pacific Theater. The telegram tersely stated, "I regret to inform you that your son Pvt. Robert Ronan was killed in action on the Island of Guadalcanal while engaging the enemy in combat. He died honorably in service to his country."

In the very bottom corner was an old hymnbook. Inside it was a picture of Robert and a newspaper clipping marking the pages of two songs, "Nearer my God to Thee" and "Near the Cross, Oh Lamb of God". Also included was the announcement of the funeral service held at the First Christian Church on Main Street. There was also the star that was displayed in the window of every home of a family who had a loved one die in World War II. Robert will always be 19 years old.

There was Nothing Fancy in Grandpa's Toolbox

Grandpa lived by himself up in the river bottom north of our place in Highland Township when I was a child. He was a farmhand on the Thompson Farm. He lived a very simple almost Amish life. His household furnishings and furniture were Spartan. His kitchen utensils and pans were meager. He wore overalls 24/7 as we say now, chambray shirts and a sweater and long johns in the winter. I can attest that he ate simple fare. I remember eating copious quantities of soup beans and corn bread, fried and boiled potatoes and a few vegetables at his table. If he had dessert it would be fruit. He was wiry as we say down home. I'm sure his income was as meager as his life style.

As you might expect reminiscent of his life style his toolbox was nothing fancy. It was a rectangular wooden box about three feet long, four inches deep and eight to ten inches wide. There was a wooden divide near one side where the saw and square were placed to protect them from damage by the other tools. The handle was a quarter inch rope attached to each end of the box.

He had two hammers in the box. The one I often used had a wooden handle and one ear or claw broken off. The handle near the head was boogered up as we said on the farm indicating that it had had some rough use through the years. The head was chipped and the edges were worn off but I loved to drive nails with it. "Drive the nail, don't push it," Grandpa would say as I struggled to hit the nail on the head.

He had an ancient handsaw that he had tied string around the handle and then taped over the string to hold it together and to prevent the crack from pinching his hand. At one time it was shiny and well used. By the time I came around it was a bit rusty and harder to use. It had not been set, sharpened, for a long time. Grandpa used to say that

171

you could worry the board into several pieces quicker than cutting it with that old saw.

He had a flat, nubbin of a carpenter pencil in the box. I called it stubby as it was about a fourth as long as when it was new. He had not used it much over the past few years of his life. I felt like a real carpenter when I drew a line with it.

Long before there were electric sanders, carpenters used a wood rasp to smooth wood. Grandpa had one. It looked like a regular file on steroids because the grooves were quite wide and the teeth were much longer.

Grandpa also had a chalk line that used blue powdered chalk to mark long lines. He also had an "L" shaped square. Isn't that an oxymoron? How can a square be shaped like an "L"? It was. I still have one. He also had a hand plane with blades somewhat like a razor to shape wood. The blades could be adjusted to take small or large cuts. It would make you eat your lunch as my dad would say.

In today's world the electric drill quickly drills holes. Grandpa had a hand powered brace and bit. It was shaped like half of a plus sign. There was a round hand grip on the top, a chuck in the bottom to hold the bits with a handle in the middle that rotated the axis of the handle and bit. It was hard and slow work but it was at the apex of technology at the time.

Carpenters of today have electric drills, planes and sanders. They use lasers to level and to measure; nail guns instead of hammers; electric saws instead of handsaws. Not when Grandpa lived. It was much more simple and plain back then.

Grandpa worked at manual labor all of his life. He knew all about hand tools and how to use them. His huge, rough and callused hands were strong yet gentle when he placed them on mine to guide the saw and work the plane. I can still see his perspiration dampened blue chambray work shirt as he toiled in the sun, his old straw hat askew on his head.

Grandpa and I used to work on projects together. I see his warm smile, feel his patience as I fumbled over work that he could do quickly and well. I have some of his old tools and I am swamped with memories when I use them. He lived a simple life that influenced me and helped make me what I am today. I miss him.

The Bloomers

Amelia Bloomer, born in about 1850, was an agent of change. Her contribution to the world was her bloomers. She began wearing a garment that consisted of a short skirt over loose fitting trousers gathered around the ankles. The outfit quickly became known as bloomers and became the rage for women engaging in athletic contests and other activities that were previously verboten because of the need for propriety and modesty. Later on the word bloomers also became interchangeable for women's undergarments, unmentionables or dainties.

In the late 1950s a pair of bloomers became the prank of choice of three rather resourceful and inventive practical jokers who just happened to be employed at the Worthington State Bank. An aside, why do we refer to a single item as a pair of underwear or a pair of pants when we never refer to a shirt as a pair of shirts? Don't say it is because there are two legs or two leg openings because a shirt has two arms or two arm openings also. It is a conundrum. To you who are still learning, that means a puzzle.

Hobert was the chief financial officer — cashier — and Jo Ellen and Betty were tellers at the bank. The bloomers in question made their first appearance at a Christmas party held in the staid confines of the auspicious, audacious bank. Jo Ellen opened a gift and there they were. Bloomers that would fit Dumbo the Elephant. They were custom made with half of the pants made of a garish red cloth with purple polka dots. The other half was green and yellow stripes. The waistband was hot pink. There was a multi-colored combination of brown, turquoise, lavender, army green and chartreuse fringe around each leg. The giver of the gift was clothed in anonymity but from the looks on the faces of two particular party revelers, the perpetrator could easily be narrowed to two suspects. The gauntlet had been thrown down and the Battle of the Bloomers was on.

One morning Betty's neighbor called her and laughingly asked, "Did you forget to take in all of your laundry last night? What is that on your clothes line?" She looked out of the window and immediately her face turned as red as the face of the Enron CEO at the congressional hearing. She slammed the phone down and ran through the dew-laden grass to the clothesline and removed the offending bloomers from their place of honor.

Hobert always parked his car beside the bank on a concrete apron that extended outward from the East Side of the bank building. There was only one parking place and everyone in town knew that he parked there. There was no more prominent location except in the middle of the triangle. He parked there one windy day after returning from lunch. At five o'clock as the bank employees were leaving for the day several people were standing and pointing in the direction of Hobert's car. He looked also and to his chagrin there were the bloomers flapping in the breeze from his radio antenna. Old Glory never flew more proudly. He drove home with the pennant jauntily waving in the breeze.

The sun shone brightly on Easter morning as Jo Ellen and Harvey stepped out of the house in their Easter finery to attend church services. Hanging in full view over the front porch steps, bouncing and waving for all to see were the delicate, dancing dainties. A sign read, "No new Easter outfit would be complete without these undergarments."

The Greene County Fair was held in Worthington and it was the social event of the summer for the county. Hundreds of people came to the weeklong fair. Betty and Ernie's son was a member of the beef cattle 4-H club. One evening, a large, laughing crowd gathered around the stall where he housed his cows. The onlookers were roaring with laughter because tacked to the wooden gate were the offending bloomers with this sign, "Try these prize winning panties on for size. I never go anywhere without mine."

Those bloomers were later seen on Jo Ellen's flag pole and hanging from a huge sunflower at Hobert's house. They later appeared as a baby shower gift and at Betty's anniversary party. The last known sighting occurred several years later when Hobert retired. He should have suspected something like this would happen. The last gift he opened at his last annual meeting with the board of directors and employees, was a beautifully wrapped box with a huge brightly colored bow.

He thanked everyone and was about to close the meeting when Betty suggested that he take a closer look at the bow. Sure enough although they were carefully contrived to look like a bow, in truth the bow was the pantaloons de jure — the Bloomers.

Push The Brakes on Huldy And You Sped Up!

We tend to remember the first time we do something. The mind is quite consistent in that aspect. There is one caveat, though. I'm not sure that an AARPER's mind is consistent on much of anything. But I digress so early in the story.

First time events that we remember are such things as the first time you kissed a girl, the first day of school especially high school and the first day of boot camp in the service. One tends to remember your wedding night, the birth of your children and the first car you ever owned.

My first car was Huldy. I loved that car! Not in the way that I love my wife and children, but guys know what I mean. Old Huldy was a 1938 Ford, four-door, eight-cylinder car with the gearshift on the floor. She was 17 years old when I bought her. Of course, being my first, it was the most memorable one I have ever owned. I purchased it between my sophomore and junior year of high school for $23.50, drove it for a couple of years and traded it in for a 1948 streamline Chevy.

Huldy was a simple car with very small windows. It had windshield wipers, an AM radio and a gasoline powered heater that never worked. There was no interior light and very few lights on the dashboard. It had mechanical brakes which meant that all of the pressure placed on the brake shoes to stop the car was determined by the strength of the leg attached to the foot that pressed on the brake pedal. When I applied the brakes, especially in an emergency situation, it seemed to me that Huldy would speed up instead of slowing down. That sensation was caused because she just didn't slow down as quickly as I expected her to. Those were the few amenities that were offered in those days so I added a few.

I painted the wheel rims in red as well as the side grillwork on the hood. On the inside I painted the dashboard red, added a steering wheel cover, and it was my dream machine; my chick mobile; my love machine. More than that, she was my ticket to independence.

Driving Huldy was a signal to the world that I was a man. In my car I was a man of the world, able to go and come at my whim and whimsy. Boys ride bicycles men drive cars. Boys walk with girls to and from events only in town, men pick up girls in their cars and take them to places out of town. Girls want to go out with men, not boys. Even though I was a "man", I know that my parents worried every time I left in that lumbering car wondering if I would return alive. I never thought about it. However, when my daughters began to drive, I worried big time about their safety.

Today, in stark contrast, we ask cars to do so many things for us. They have messages programmed in a computer to tell us when to add water and gasoline, and when to have the car serviced. Some cars even have a spoken message to tell the driver when the door is ajar. We are cooled and heated to a specified level for optimum comfort. **(An Aside**: It is most perplexing to me but I have noticed that BW closes the heat outlets in the winter because they produce too much heat and in the summer time she closes them because the air conditioner produces too much cold air. This is one of life's many mysteries that the male brain cannot discern.) My car sends a message when the tire pressure is low. How cool is that? Cars tell us how many miles we are getting per gallon of fuel, how many more miles we can go with the existing fuel, and who has removed his shoes in the back seat.

Further, we ask cars to play CD's, FM and AM radio, tape decks and run radar detectors. Also, we open the trunk and the fuel tank access door from inside the car. The car locks the doors automatically when the shift lever is engaged. The seat moves to just the right position for the driver and passengers. Interior lights are positioned at the greatest angle and location for passenger convenience. The headlights are turned on and off automatically. The brakes adjust themselves. The rear view mirror adjusts to night driving and the outside mirrors are adjusted from inside the car. Some outside mirrors are heated to prevent snow and ice buildup. Turn signals tell others when we are going to turn, if we remember to use them. A computer chip tells us what is malfunctioning and what should be repaired. The steering wheel is adjustable. There is a place to hold your drinking container while driving. There are heating coils in the rear window to prevent and remove ice and snow. "My car also has a port in the dash where my wife plugs in her cell phone and charges it as we motor along. It can also power a small vacuum cleaner if needed. We don't have one, but how cool is that?"

Isn't it amazing what services cars provide and I haven't listed everything? However, my '38 Ford had something that my new Buick does not have and never will have. It had a Babe Magnet installed in the front seat. I know that is not politically correct but remember that was when I was *Lost in The Fifties Tonight*. Besides she was my first.

Being A Parent Is The Hardest Job I Ever Had

Some of you who are a bit long in the tooth can remember back in the very late 50s and 60s and perhaps into the early 70s when an ulcer was the badge of honor. It was an affliction shared by harried business people and professionals. Those so afflicted bragged endlessly at cocktail parties about their aching, acid-filled, ulcerated stomachs. There was a bizarre status associated with the severity of the extant ulcer. Maalox was the "drug of choice" at company gatherings. It flowed like a river of relief down the esophagus to sooth the churning volcanic acid.

If you did not have an ulcer you were not a committed hard-nosed, career driven, company man who put work and career before all other obligations. If you did not have an ulcer you were a slacker. You weren't trying hard enough. You worked in a dead-end job on the back streets of Nowhereville. You lived on a dead end alley with no access to the boulevard of success. People don't talk about ulcers any more.

Today the topic of conversation over lunch at Bob's "Gravy on Everything" Café is stress. After work coworkers go to the local pub and kibitz about the boss and the workload at Cubicle City. A frequent topic of discussion is burnout.

There is no job that is more demanding than being a husband or wife and a parent. There is no career that requires greater commitment. There is no occupation that requires as much attention to detail. There is no position on the corporate ladder that requires more continual responsibility.

Many jobs and careers are stressful. However, I suggest that you do not know stress until you walk the floor at night holding your child who is unable to sleep because of an illness knowing that there is nothing you can do about it.

Stress is not knowing how to referee a fight between your child and the "monster kid" down the street who is impossible to deal with. Stress is dealing with the first day of school and seeing your child take the first steps away from you. Stress is not knowing when to fight for your child and when to let the child fight his own battles. Stress is dealing with sibling rivalry. Stress is coping with a hormone driven adolescent who is major league defiant and lashes out toward every restriction invoked for his or her own good, no matter how benignant, mild and kind it is.

Many jobs require a strong commitment of time. Some professions require immensely more than others if you are going to climb the ladder of success and make it in America. Many parents brag about the long hours they put in on the job and in their commute. They leave the house before the children get up and come home after they are in bed. "But I make a good living," is their counterpoint to justify the neglect of their family.

I suggest to you that parenting is a 24/7 time commitment from the time you birth a child until that child leaves your home to create his or her own home. The commitment continues even after that until it is time for your page to be ripped out of the book of life. Your own dreams just might have to sit in the corner gathering dust, but many will not deprive themselves to help others even their children.

Many careers require high levels of responsibility to provide services and manufacture products. That is without disputation. However, when you are totally responsible for every aspect in the life of one or more children, that is responsibility. It never ends.

Many jobs require time which deprives one of sleep and rest. I suggest that you do not know sleep deprivation until you care for an infant's every need day and night. Babies do not care whether you are rested or not. They are unaware that you have needs. Their only concern is getting their needs met, instantly, night or day. I remember the disorientation that resulted at times by tending our babies deep into the night.

There are those who will vehemently disagree with my assessment of parenting. They will say their job is more stressful, requires more time and responsibility and creates more stress than their role of parenting. If you, dear reader, are one of those who feel that way then I will state gently that you are not parenting properly. You are probably depending upon a spouse or relative to assume much of your role as a parent. Or, you are paying someone else to rear your child while you pursue your career. Of course your career or job is more demanding because you have made it the priority of your life instead of your family. That seems to be the American way and it is so sad.

Where Did That Come From?

There are two wonderfully poignant songs that tell the story of passing time. One is "Turn Around" and the other is "Sunrise Sunset" from Fiddler on the Roof. Both songs tell the melodramatic story of parents with children who suddenly grow up before their eyes. They are children today, adults tomorrow. Reminiscent of the ambiance and sentiment of those songs I have noticed sudden changes in my life. They sneaked up on me like age, fat and old underwear.

One day I noticed that there was hair growing out of my ears. It looked like a fox had gone into its den and left the end of its tail sticking out. About the same time I noticed that the hair in my nose had grown out and down to my upper lip. My nose looks like a walrus nose. Then I noticed that my eyebrows had grown very bushy and large and they flapped up and down like windshield wipers on an 18-wheeler. That is really unfair.

In the past only old men had those problems. I have lost the hair off the top of my head but I have gained much more than I need or want on my torso — front and back. Who wrote the action plan for that move? I am thinking about letting the hair grow out of my nose and ears then tie it in a bow over the top of my head to cover my baldness.

One day I noticed that some of my fingernails had changed. Instead of being smooth and supple, now they are brittle and have ridges and rows in them. They look like a concrete sidewalk that was smoothed with a garden rake.

Last week BW and I went to the matinee movie. I noticed that I had a place on my right elbow that hurt every time I put it down on the seat arm. Later I looked at it and it looked like a scrape or perhaps I had had a giant blister that popped and exposed the dermis. I thought for about ten hours and could not remember when or how it happened. I have also noticed that when we go to the theater or a movie, the actors do not speak as loudly or as clearly as they once did. Whom do I speak to about that?

I can't see my belt anymore but I still wear the same size pants. Of course they fit a little lower than they once did, just above my knees.

Four years ago I had to get glasses. Now I have two pairs with the lines in them. I use one pair to see and another pair to use while working at the computer. They are not very interchangeable. I mistakenly wore the computer pair to work one day and had great difficulty seeing beyond the length of my forearm. And then there is weight.

Fat sneaks up on you too. I have three sizes of clothing in my closet: Extra Large, Extra Extra Large and You've Got to be Kidding! I wear all of them depending on how much I weigh at the moment. They are all in good condition because they receive so little wearing time. I move through all three sizes about as often as Israel moves through the towns in the West Bank.

Lately I have noticed that I make two or three trips to Ft. Necessity, if you know what I mean, during the night. That is why there are about 89 nightlights on in our house all the time. One night a small airplane mistook our house for the runway light and almost landed on the roof. And it wasn't even December 24. And medicine.

When I was a kid old people took medicine every day, not young people like me. Well, lately I comprehended that since my cardiac event I take an aspirin in the morning and Lipitor at night to control my cholesterol level. When did that happen?

I have a mirror in the second drawer of the vanity in the bathroom that I share with the washer and dryer. The other day I pulled the drawer open and leaned down to get the mirror and hairbrush. I could see my reflection and in horror I watched as all the skin and fat on my face flopped downward until it looked like I was wearing a parka made of skin. My face looked like a worried basset hound. Recoiling in horror I blurted, "Who is that?" All together now:

Turn around and you're young, turn around and you groan, Turn around and you can't make the stairs on your own.

Old Friends Are Special

I visited with some old friends today. Old friends make you feel comfortable. They are an attachment to the past, an affirmation of the present and they provide stability for the future. These friends are on dad and mom's farm that they bought in 1941.

BW and I trekked through the woods searching for the elusive fungi known as morel mushrooms. It is an annual spring ritual that many Hoosiers follow. We stopped by a huge beech tree that has been a farm landmark all of my life. It has anchored the north side of the woods on the fence line between the old Thompson farm and us. It has stood there since long before I came into this world. It stands as a sentinel at the top of the bluff. Dad would say that something was just beyond that big beech tree and I would know exactly where he was talking about. When I was very short in the tooth Dad said, "See those letters carved there, Ike Bollinger did that a long time ago." Today, I could still read Bollinger although the letters have been distorted as the tree has grown. It is probably because I know what the letters are. Each time I visit it is more difficult to read but I had to say hello to my old friend.

There is a pastureland of 15 - 20 acres through the woods that we call the open field. It has supplied browse for the cows and horses for many years. At one time Dad had a pond there and a single tree stood guard beside it. Both have faded into the mist of memory. Many times Brother and I heaved our little Western Flyer carrying our tent and supplies to the open field. Mom supplied our food. What joys we had camping under the star canopy listening to the whippoorwill calls and the hooting owls as the blanket of darkness was pulled over the western sky.

The open field was also the site of a traumatic incident. Dad was tilling the ground with the tractor. My job was to control the burn-off of sagebrush. I thought the fire was going to get into the woods and I was terrified. Dad came just in the nick of time and we put the fire out. I think about those things as I stand in the open field.

A creek rises from the area of the open field and runs down through the woods to the river. It only runs during the rainy seasons. Brother and I used to go up there in the hot summer time and play in the small pools of water. There is an outcropping of sandstone that the stream flows over. Dad said that when the original house was built, the builders carved foundation stones from those rocks. The house still sits on those stones that sit on top of the ground. We spent many an hour on the cool, smooth, slippery stone. We carved our initials in the stones that remain to this day. Mysteriously, during the dry seasons, the water disappears into a subterranean grotto at that spot.

Along the way is the place where Dad taught us how to find slippery elm trees and chew the inner bark. I can still feel the slippery, slimy, flavorless substance that was somewhat like chewing gum. Near there, Dad showed us how to climb small hickory trees then lean from side to side to bend them like circus performers. That provided fun and diversion for two rag-a-muffin farm kids. They are so large now that even as much as I weigh I couldn't bend them over anymore.

Just down over the bluff beyond the big beech tree I sat on a log and reminisced. There is a group of hickory trees standing together like relatives at a family reunion. They have been there longer than I have. It is the place where Dad and I went squirrel hunting on one memorable morning. The sun was just rising over the hills as we slipped Indian-like through the woods until we were right under the trees. The squirrels were having a banquet in the tree canopy. As they ate hickory nuts, they chewed off the shell and the cuttings or shavings were falling like rain drops.

We had a 12-gauge pump shotgun and a single shot .22 rifle. Dad quietly gave me the shotgun and whispered, "I am going to shake this sapling and they will run. Get ready to shoot." I took my stance and was ready but I was not quite ready for what happened next. He shook the tree and the squirrels scattered like leaves before the wind. There must have been at least a gazillion squirrels rampaging through the treetops. I didn't know which one to shoot. Just as quickly as they appeared they disappeared into nests and dens but not before Dad got one with the rifle. Dad asked, "Son, why didn't you shoot?" Almost tearfully I said, "I didn't know where to shoot there were too many of them. I didn't know what to do." He chuckled and said, "Well, we'll get a bunch of them next time." We sat down under the trees and with a wistful, far away look in his eyes, he told me that he and his dad had a similar experience when he was a little tasker. Since our cover was blown, we trouped back to the house. We still had squirrel for breakfast the next morning. We had the one Dad got that morning and two more he took in the evening of the same day.

Just beyond those trees is the spot where Kenny, the older neighborhood boy, taught Brother and me how to crush leaves, roll them into a piece of brown paper sack and make a cigar. We smoked one and it didn't take long. They burn quickly. We went home and Mom noticed right away that we had been smoking. It is hard to disguise what you have been doing when you smell like burning leaves. The dance was over. Well, not yet, there was more dancing when Dad applied the peach tree tea to certain anatomical parts. That was the first and last time we did that.

Neither BW nor I found any morels that day but I enjoyed being back home to spend some time with old friends.

Win and Sam: Lost In the '40s

Winfred and Samantha sat rocking and reminiscing on the porch of the inn at McCormick's Creek State Park. It was the summer of 1992. Their white wicker rockers were time machines that transported them back to that idyllic summer when they met. They were two young people thrown together by the winds of fate. Cupid shot an entire quiver of arrows straight into their hearts and they could not recover from the wounds of love that he inflicted upon them.

It was a hot and humid day at "The Creek", the same kind of day as that fateful day in 1946. Win sat in the huge rocking chair, his eyes closed, his head tilted back. As he gently rocked, his mind raced back through the years to that summer. He reached back and pulled out the index card from the file cabinet in his memory that recorded the first time he ever saw Samantha — Sam. That day was forever branded into his memory. It was an imprint like a branding iron on the hip of a longhorn steer that would not wear off or fade away. Sam sat with him, lost in reverie, a knowing smile flitted across the miles recorded in her face.

Indiana summers are noted for their tendency to be uncomfortable. It is a farm state situated in the climate that meteorologists call humid continental. Massive yields of corn and soybeans are grown there that become major food items for humans as well as animals. Hoosiers like to say that corn and soybeans love what humans do not and that is high heat and humidity.

"The Creek" is a popular summer destination for families who come to the park to enjoy the quietude and to escape the heat and humidity of the city and town. Many young families were in the park on this day. The swimming pool is located a short distance from the inn, across a meadow of lush grass dotted with trees and picnic tables. It was a busy place. Children and a few parents splashed about seeking respite from the heat. The water in the pool at "The Creek" is always cool even on the hottest days. Some say it is cold.

.   The meadow was alive with activity. Towering hickory, tulip poplar, sycamore and maple trees surround it. Children played with Frisbees and on the nearby playground equipment consisting mainly of swings and slides. Some older people played croquet and a sandlot game of softball was underway. The smell of charcoal, hot dogs and hamburgers permeated the air as families prepared picnic lunches.

The horse barn beyond the meadow and through the woods was almost empty. The horses had expressed their preference to remain in the barn or in the shade. They had expressed their reluctance with snorts and stamping when they were led out and saddled. Young and old riders pretended to be cowboys in the old west or co-conspirators of Robin Hood and his merry band as they rode their noble steeds through the tranquil woods. Some of the more aggressive and physically fit families hiked along the trails in the woods. White puffy clouds meandered across the sky like a herd of sheep looking for grass. The air was fragrant with the scent of the newly mown lawn.

The Bloomington High School class of 1942 was holding its fiftieth reunion at the inn. A sea of gray splashed on the shores of time as they reminisced about school events plucked from the mists of yesterday. Song birds warbled, crows clamored and doves mournfully cooed from the nearby trees. A few diurnal raccoons foraged for crayfish, tadpoles, and other delicacies along McCormick's Creek.

Amidst it all, Winfred and Samantha were in another world. They were not in the class of '42 but "The Creek" had a special meaning for them. More than forty years had passed since they were here. The blustery winds of 66 winters had blown through Win's clothing. What hair he had left was a frosty stubble of shrubbery surrounding the vacant field on the top of his head. He was of medium stature and the years had brought along a few extra pounds that congregated around his waist. His eyes twinkled through wire-rimmed glasses. His face bore a look of mischievous intelligence as he and Sam leaned together and talked in low voices. Win said, "You know, Sam, it was no accident, that I met you. There was a plan in place by someone greater that caused us to meet. I believe that with all of my heart."

Sam said wistfully, "I think you are right Win. It just seems like it was yesterday when we met. Where have the years gone?" A smile crossed her face as that memory lingered in her mind.

Sam was elegant and jovial. She was nearly as tall as Winfred. Her once honey blonde hair was now brindle colored, gray mixed with the blonde. Her eyes crinkled and her mouth turned upward as another smile of remembrance danced across her face. Occasionally she would reach over and pat Win on the knee or avert her glance downward as if a bit embarrassed with the conversation. It was obvious that in her youth she was drop dead gorgeous. She had the kind of beauty that when she walked into a room, men would give her the once over two or three times. She too carried a few more pounds around the equator. Her quiet laughter was of a contented person approaching three score and five.

Win chuckled and said, "You were just a country girl, right off the farm in Bee Hunter, Indiana. In fact, I don't think you were even wearing shoes when I first saw you." He squinted and laughed as Sam pretended to be offended by his remark.

"Well, you were not much better," she mocked, "Spencer was not exactly a huge metropolis. It still isn't. You were just a small potato from a small town that named its high school mascot "Cops" because the center of America's population was near the town at the time. Some

Hick Town that was. It was called a jerk water town because the train only stopped there once a week." Win laughed, slapped his knee and said, "Now that hurt. I am offended by that remark. I don't deny it I'm just offended by it."

Sam did grow up on a farm near the rural community of Bee Hunter, Indiana, and she was a long time 4-H member and country girl. Prior to the 1940's women had few opportunities or need to work outside of the home but W.W. II had changed all of that. The working landscape and job climate changed. The doors of opportunity, born of necessity, opened for women to enter the work force. They went to work in record numbers in offices, factories and business. That was what propelled Sam to be working at "The Creek" as a waitress in the Inn.

Winfred was indeed a townie who grew up in the neighborhood of "The Creek" in the small town of Spencer, Indiana. His grandparents and an uncle and aunt were farmers in the area. He spent most every summer working on the farm as he grew to manhood in the years 1938-44. Farm work then was mostly manual labor especially on the small farms in Owen County. He helped put up hay, milked cows, worked the garden, planted, cultivated and shucked corn and tended hogs. When there was slack time he and his grandfather and uncle built and repaired fences and cut firewood for the winter. He also worked on weekends and vacation times during the school year.

Win was stocky and strong because he worked so hard. In the summer of 1944, after high school graduation he enlisted in the Marine Corps. He was about five feet ten inches tall and 170 pounds of muscle. At Boot Camp in Parris Island, South Carolina, he grew another inch and added 20 pounds of muscle to his sturdy frame. As soon as boot camp was over, his company was shipped out to the Pacific. His outfit joined the island hopping campaign of the South Pacific Theater of operations.

Island by island the allied forces pressed closer and closer to the Imperial Japanese homeland of Japan. The Japanese forces had to know, by this time, that the war was lost as the allied forces pushed relentlessly onward through the islands of Wake, The Marshalls, Kwajalein, Eniwetok, Truk, Guadalcanal, the Solomons, Guam, Saipan, the Marianas, Iwo Jima the Philippines and Okinawa. However, they fought fiercely with a fanaticism of unequalled fervor inflicting horrendous casualties on the allied armed forces.

In April and June of 1945, Win's outfit was engaged in the battle for Okinawa, which was 370 miles, about the length of the state of Indiana, and the last stop before Japan. The battle began on April 1. The Japanese fought with suicidal fury on land and sea. They lost over 3,500 airplanes through their kamikaze suicide missions and 110,000 men plus an additional 7,800 taken as prisoners. The allies suffered 50,000 casualties on land and sea before the battle ended in late June.

Win's outfit suffered severe casualties. It was during that battle that Win was wounded and sent to the rear where he recuperated and rejoined his outfit in August. He was awarded the Purple Heart and the Distinguished Service Medal for bravery and recognition of service beyond the call of duty. He was on the Island of Okinawa on August 6, 1945 when the first atomic bomb was dropped on Hiroshima and on August 9 when the second bomb was dropped on Nagasaki. The war ended on September 2. His unit remained in Japan and was assigned to the staff of Gen. Douglas MacArthur and the army of occupation. He was rotated home in the spring of 1946.

That summer, he was a blonde, muscular, tanned G.I. just back from W.W. II. After he had enjoyed the adulation of several celebrations for his service during the war, he realized that he must now find a job. A friend was working at "The Creek" and recommended him to be a lifeguard and pool manager. He was hired and therein begins the tale of Win and Sam.

One day Win was eating lunch at the Inn. He noticed a tall, stunningly beautiful waitress and part-time night manager of the restaurant. Her smile would melt Hard Hearted Hannah's heart. She could make Scrooge smile. Her blonde hair shone like sunlight in the late afternoon. Her laughter sounded like clinking crystal glasses or a wind chime on a soft summer evening. Her deep blue eyes were tantalizing. He screwed up his courage and introduced himself. He said, "Hi, my name is Winfred but my friends call me Win." She smiled demurely and replied, "My name is Samantha and my friends call me Sam." From that day forward he found many reasons to be at the Inn.

As they sat on the porch, this day in 1992, Win chuckled and said, "Remember how we used to meet and talk at the huge rock down by the creek in the evenings? That old rock is still there. I saw it as we came into the park."

Sam winked and reminisced about how they would sneak down to the stables and ride the horses late at night. She smilingly admitted, "I also remember two crazy kids who would sneak off down to the pool on moonlight nights and go swimming under the stars. That was so romantic. The stars twinkled so brightly and they seemed close enough to touch. There were so many lightning bugs that their lights were like tiny flashlights on the path." Win added, "I remember that old Indian blanket we would spread out on the wet grass and how we talked endlessly, and, and how you would bring leftover food from the kitchen and we would eat until we would almost burst. Ah, yes, those were the days."

Win said, "Sam, I have to tell you that you had the sweetest kisses this side of Hershey, Pennsylvania. I was caught in the gale force winds of Hurricane Samantha and blown off course. I was a great swimmer but I drowned in your deep blue eyes."

Sam smiled coyly, pinched Win's cheek and murmured, "You always were a sweet talker, Win Sandler. And, you had the cutest smile I had ever seen and you were so polite and considerate. You were downright irresistible. Once I dabbled my toe in Lake Sandler, I was hooked." The rocking chairs creaked as they rocked and reminisced.

Win enrolled that fall at Indiana University under the G.I. Bill. Two summers later they married and began their married life in Vet Village, a conglomeration of small green house trailers on the Northwest side of the campus. They both worked while Win completed his degree.

America was once again at war in the Far East — Korea — when Win graduated in 1950. The state department was looking for the right kind of people to serve in overt and covert missions in the interest of America around the world. Naturally they came looking for Win. He was a natural — a decorated veteran who was intelligent and made excellent grades in history and political science. They offered him a position and he accepted. He graduated on Saturday and went to work the following Monday.

He worked in the Foreign Service Stateside as well as in Europe and the Far East. Very few people knew that Win was involved in many highly secret missions. He was an unlikely looking espionage specialist but he served his country in exemplary fashion throughout the Cold War period. He fulfilled assignments in Japan, Germany, Vietnam, Russia and Austria.

During this time, Win and Sam were blessed with three children. As time drifted by them as we all know it can, the children grew up, graduated from universities, married and blessed Win and Sam with six grandchildren. Their ties with Indiana became less and less. After 45 years of service to America, Win retired. He and Sam did not return to live in Indiana but chose to remain in the Shenandoah Valley of

Virginia near two of their children and five of their grandchildren.

During this particularly hot and sultry week in August, however, they were revisiting the place where they met when they stood on the front end of life. They were reliving those times when the world was young and they were so much in love and everything was possible. The world was within their grasp and nothing stood in their way that they could not overcome.

Today, they stood on the back end of life and tallied the balance sheet. The sweet, lovely memories of a happy and blessed lifetime together far outnumbered the unhappy and negative aspects that are a part of everyone's journey through time.

Today, they were oblivious to all of the other activities at "The Creek." In their minds they could hear Glen Miller's Band playing *In The Mood* and the Andrews Sisters singing *Apple Blossom Time*. They were lost in the Forties.

."

ABOUT THE AUTHOR

Dr. Larry Vandeventer grew up on the banks of White River on a small farm beyond Dead Horse Creek, North of Calvertville, Indiana.

He and BW are proud "Ramblers", graduates of Worthington-Jefferson High School, Worthington, Indiana. The have two married daughters, Kristi and Sharla and one granddaughter, Audrey.

He is a veteran of the U.S. Navy and a former full-time minister as well as a teacher, high school assistant principal, principal and superintendent. Presently, he serves as a professor in the Graduate Education Department of Indiana Wesleyan University. And he writes a weekly column for two newspapers in Indiana.

He recently published his first book titled, *Bumps In The Road [Things I Have Run Across]*.